FIRES OF ST. JOHN

A DRAMA IN FOUR ACTS
FROM THE GERMAN OF

HERMANN SUDERMANN

*Author of "Magda," "The Joy
of Living," "Sodom's End," Etc.*

AS PRESENTED FOR THE FIRST TIME
ON THE AMERICAN STAGE IN
BOSTON ON JANUARY
TWENTY-FIRST
NINETEEN
HUNDRED
&
4

Translated and Adapted
by CHARLES SWICKARD

BOSTON, JOHN W. LUCE
and COMPANY, 1904

COPYRIGHT NOTICE and WARRNING

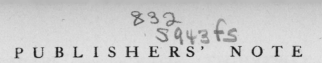

PUBLISHERS' NOTE

¶ THIS translation and adaptation of " JOHANNISFEUER " was made by special permission from Herr SUDERMANN, and is the only authorized English version.

¶ BY arrangement with the publishers, Miss NANCE O'NEIL, who first produced this play in English, as here given, will continue to use Mr. Swickard's adaptation exclusively.

FIRES OF ST. JOHN

WAS FIRST PRESENTED IN ENGLISH, IN BOSTON, MASSACHUSETTS, ON JANUARY TWENTY-FIRST, 1904, WITH THE FOLLOWING CAST

MR. BRAUER	MR. GEORGE C. STALEY
MRS. BRAUER	MRS. CHARLES W. BROOKS
GERTRUDE	MISS BLANCHE STODDARD
GEORGE VON HARTEN .	MR. E. J. RATCLIFFE
AN OLD GYPSY WOMAN .	MISS RICCA ALLEN
HAFFNER	MR. NORWELL McGREGOR
MR. PAUL	MR. FREDERICK SULLIVAN
KATIE	MISS FANNIE CANNON
and	
MARIE	MISS NANCE O'NEIL

CAST OF CHARACTERS

MR. BRAUER . . . . Proprietor of a large country estate

MRS. BRAUER . . . . His wife

GERTRUDE . . . . Their daughter

GEORGE VON HARTEN. . . . . Their nephew

AN OLD GYPSY WOMAN

HAFFNER . . . . Assistant Pastor

MR. PAUL. . . . . Overseer

KATIE . . . . Housekeeper

SERVANT GIRL

and

MARIE . . . . A Foundling

Time of action, about 1880

Place of action, Pomerania (Prussia)

THE FIRES OF ST. JOHN

ACT ONE

*Breakfast-room at the Brauer residence. The back
wall is formed by three glass doors, separated by
marble pillars. Behind this, the veranda is visible,
and balustrade, hung with fine rug, and stairs,
leading into the garden. The glass doors have
practical, solid wooden shutters, with bars, fast-
ening inside. Doors R. and L. Large table C.
with breakfast laid Front, to the left, sofa, table
and easy-chair. To the right, sewing-machine,
and basket filled with table-linen. Old-fashioned
photos and engravings on walls. Otherwise,
well-to-do family home.*

Time of day: Morning.

[GERTRUDE *busy at breakfast-table.*]

BRAUER.

[*Enters with* PAUL, *from R.*] Confound it! Everything seems to go wrong this morning!

[*Throws his cap on chair, angrily.*]

GERTRUDE.

[*Happily.*] Good-morning, papa!

[11]

THE FIRES OF ST. JOHN

BRAUER.

Morning, my child. Such carelessness! You ought to be ashamed of yourself. If this thing had happened earlier in the season, out on the meadows — but at this time of the year —!!! Oh! Confound it all, anyway!!!!! It is inexcusable!!!

GERTRUDE.

What is the matter, papa?

BRAUER.

The black cow has been overfed. But of course, when Marie is not about to look after everything, things go to rack and ruin. Well, man, what excuse are you going to make?

PAUL.

None, Mr. Brauer.

BRAUER.

Now that's the most sensible thing you have said this morning. Here, take a cigar and get to work; but mind! send for the veterinary surgeon at once. Have you had breakfast?

PAUL.

Yes, sir!

BRAUER.

Then what the devil are you waiting for?

PAUL.

I — I — I wanted to excuse myself, and ——

BRAUER.

[*Impatiently.*] It's all right! it's all right!

PAUL.

[*Remains — hesitatingly.*] G — Good-morning!!

BRAUER.

Well?

THE FIRES OF ST. JOHN

PAUL.

I — I have something else to tell you ——

BRAUER.

Then out with it.

PAUL.

[*With a glance at* GERTRUDE.] But ——

BRAUER.

H'm! Gertrude, darling, will you please see if it is still threatening rain?

GERTRUDE.

Yes, papa! [*Goes out on the veranda.*]

BRAUER

Well?

PAUL.

[*Confidentially.*] The old hag has turned up again.

BRAUER,

[*Alarmed.*] Wha —— The devil you say! H'm! Who — who has seen her?

PAUL.

She was seen begging in the village — and last night, one of my men observed her creeping stealthily around the sheds yonder.

BRAUER.

[*Scratching his head.*] Yes, yes! I had almost forgotten. She has served her last sentence — fully five years! — we have been free from her annoying presence and now, she has returned. Well, what does she want?

PAUL.

She has heard her daughter is about to be married, she says.

BRAUER.

[*Laughs.*] *Her* daughter? ha, ha! I see! no doubt she has learned of Gertrude's betrothal. Well? and ——

PAUL.

And so she has come to get her share of the wedding-cake — so she says; but she dare not venture here.

BRAUER.

Well, I should advise her to keep a respectful distance. Take good care, Mr. Paul, that she approaches no one of this house. Do you hear? No one. I will see the constable myself; and perhaps we'll soon get rid of her again. Good-morning.

PAUL.

Good-morning, Mr. Brauer.   [*Exit.*]

GERTRUDE.

[*Enters.*]   Shall I pour your coffee, papa?

BRAUER.

What? My little one looking after the breakfast, eh? Can you do all that?

GERTRUDE.

Oh papa! if I couldn't do even that ——

BRAUER.

But Marie?

GERTRUDE.

Oh, of course — not as well as she — you must have patience with me, papa!

BRAUER.

Why certainly, my pet! [*Embraces her.*]   And now, let me see — how many days are you left to me?

THE FIRES OF ST. JOHN

GERTRUDE.

Only four more days, papa.

BRAUER.

Now, you rascal! must you leave me? must you go and marry, eh? must you?

GERTRUDE.

But papa, dear, it is all your own arrangement!

BRAUER.

Of course, of course! what is a poor old man to do? Have you seen George this morning? [GERTRUDE *shakes her head.*] Such sloth! He does nothing but sleep, sleep, sleep.

GERTRUDE.

He worked until very late last night, papa. At dawn this morning I saw his light still burning; and then it was past three o'clock.

BRAUER.

Yes, I must admit, he is diligent and industrious — but also stubborn — damned stubborn. [*The last is said almost to himself. Aloud.*] Has mama been down?

GERTRUDE.

No, not yet.

BRAUER.

And Marie? has she returned?

GERTRUDE.

She arrived by the early morning train.

BRAUER.

And how nearly finished is the lover's nest, eh?

GERTRUDE.

Only one more trip to the city, I believe she said.

THE FIRES OF ST. JOHN

BRAUER.

Well, and do you like the arrangement?

GERTRUDE.

I don't know, papa dear. I am kept entirely in the dark. It is to be a surprise to me. Oh, I will like it very much indeed, I think.

BRAUER.

And are you happy, my pet?

GERTRUDE.

Oh, papa, dear, I sometimes feel as if I didn't deserve all this happiness.

BRAUER.

Well, my dear, a housewife who calls these soft-boiled eggs, certainly does not deserve such happiness.

GERTRUDE.

[*Embarrassed.*] I only boiled them about three-quarters of an hour ——

BRAUER.

Ha, ha, ha, ha!

GERTRUDE.

Oh, I beg your pardon, papa, I will ——

BRAUER.

There, there, I was only joking; never mind it. And Marie, I suppose, is taking her rest now?

GERTRUDE.

If she only would do so. Papa, you must compel her to take a rest. No one can endure such a strain. One day she is looking after this house, and the next day she is in the city, furnishing our new home; and the nights she passes on the train. I am sure she will break down.

BRAUER.

Well, well, I will look after that.

THE FIRES OF ST. JOHN

MRS. BRAUER.

[*Enters from L.*]   Good-morning!

BRAUER.

Morning!   Well?

GERTRUDE.

[*Throws her arms around her mother.*]   Good-morning, mama dear!

MRS. BRAUER.

[*Caressing her.*]   My sweet! my pet! only four more good-mornings, and then ——

GERTRUDE.

You must come to visit me soon, mama!

MRS. BRAUER.

[*Crying.*]   Visit? ah, yes!

BRAUER.

No tears now, no tears, I beg of you!   Tears on an empty stomach — b-r-r-r-r-r, that's poison.

MRS. BRAUER.

My darling, who dressed your hair last night?

GERTRUDE.

The housekeeper.

MRS. BRAUER.

There!   I knew Marie could not have done that. But do you know — Marie — a few moments ago I opened her door softly, to see how she was resting, and found her still fully dressed, just as she came from the train, seated at the open window, a book in her lap, and staring out into space.

BRAUER.

Well, well, well!   I thought her passion for novels had passed away long ago.

MRS. BRAUER.

I've been thinking — we must watch her more closely.

THE FIRES OF ST. JOHN

BRAUER.

She needs no one to watch over her! She is well able to take care of herself; but we must spare her ——

MRS. BRAUER.

But, Henry, just now — three days before the wedding — who could think of sparing one's self?

BRAUER.

Well, you know — h'm ——

MRS. BRAUER.

Henry, you know how I love the girl; but, good gracious, she is not our own dear, sweet one ——

GERTRUDE.

Oh, she is more than that, mama dear.

MRS. BRAUER.

You are entirely too modest, my darling.

GERTRUDE.

Well, just imagine, mama dear, she was going to be married — and I remained at home ——

MRS. BRAUER.

Then we would retain our sunshine, our consolation, our —— [*Looking at breakfast-table with a questioning expression.*] But, children, I can't understand ——

GERTRUDE.

What, mama dear?

MRS. BRAUER.

Gracious! Everything is so — so —— [*Topsy-turvy indicated by action.*] If she is not going to sleep, she may as well come down here ——

GERTRUDE.

[*Laughingly caressing her mama.*] There, you see, mama, dear, not even a single meal can you eat without her.

[18]

THE FIRES OF ST. JOHN

[GEORGE VON HARTEN *enters.*]

BRAUER.

Well, at last you have aroused yourself; you ——

GEORGE.

[*Interrupts him, tapping his hand.*] There, softly, softly, dear uncle; don't begin scolding so early in the morning.

BRAUER.

Don't you think it's pretty near time to call me father, my boy?

GEORGE.

Not until after the wedding, dear uncle. Good-morning, auntie. [*Kissing her hand.*] Well, little one? [*Kissing her.*]

GERTRUDE.

[*Leans on him lovingly.*] My George. [*Laughs suddenly.*] Oh, just look! he is simply covered with hay!

GEORGE.

Then you may make yourself useful by brushing me off.

BRAUER.

The hayloft seems to be your favorite sleeping-place lately.

GEORGE.

Sleep? Heavens! who could sleep in this weather? I roam about, Lord knows where, over meadows and fields. Such St. John days!!! It's enough to drive one mad. The days never seem to end. Late last night I was sitting in front of my window. Said I to myself: "No sleep for me to-night, until that cursed nightingale runs out of melody" — when suddenly a meadow-lark announces the break of day — and there,

[19]

it's morning. To the left, the twilight: to the right, the dawn, peacefully together. From glow to glow a new day arises. Children, I tell you, it was beautiful. Give me a cup of coffee.

BRAUER.

But, tell me! Are you going to remain here now?

GEORGE.

Why, certainly, until after the wedding.

BRAUER.

But the propriety of such a thing ——

GERTRUDE.

[*Imploringly*.] Oh, papa dear ——

GEORGE.

Its immaterial to me. Under no circumstances do I desire to offend your sense of propriety; but then I will stay down at the inn, as the nearest place.

BRAUER.

And in the morning you will bring us the house full of fleas.

MRS. BRAUER.

But, Henry ——

BRAUER.

Well, it's so.

GEORGE.

If you will allow me! The wedding was set for the twentieth; therefore I obtained my first furlough from the nineteenth — and I trust you realize that I can't change the dates to suit myself. I arrived on the twentieth — and the wedding, of course — it was postponed.

MRS. BRAUER.

But, George dear, neither your home, nor anything else was ready.

GEORGE.

And besides, where am I to go? My own home is broken up; Marie has had everything torn up. By the way, has she returned?

GERTRUDE.

[*Nods.*]

MRS. BRAUER.

Why, what's the matter? Have you two had another quarrel?

GEORGE.

No, certainly not; but I should not have allowed the girl to make a drudge of herself for my sake. I almost wish I had remained at home.

GERTRUDE.

Why, she is not doing all this for your sake, but for mine.

GEORGE.

Now there, don't be conceited.

MRS. BRAUER.

[*Caressing her.*] I think she has cause to be conceited.

GEORGE.

As my future wife, she certainly has cause to be that.

BRAUER.

There, there, don't you overrate yourself.

GEORGE.

I don't, dear uncle; I am too practical for that.

BRAUER.

So, so, you are too practical, eh? then what the devil possessed you to leave this piece of paper on my desk? eh?

GEORGE.

Uncle, I beg of you, don't let us begin quarreling so early in the day.

BRAUER.

[*Angry still.*]   Very well, but what does it mean?

GEORGE.

It is simply a statement of my affairs.   I am a free and independent man, and that is to show you that I am not only willing but also able to properly support my wife.

BRAUER.

[*Still worked up.*]   But I tell you ——

MARIE.

[*Enters R.*]   Oh — pardon me, papa — good-morning!

GERTRUDE.

[*Throws arms around her.*]   Marie!

MARIE.

[*Kisses her.*]   My darling!

[*She goes to* BRAUER *and kisses his hand.*]

BRAUER.

You are back all right, I see!   Here, here!   [*Puts hand under her chin.*]   Head thrown back, I say — why, what's the matter? anything gone wrong with you, eh?

MARIE.

[*Uncertain.*]   N — no!

BRAUER.

[*To his wife.*]   Look at her — she is positively livid.

MRS. BRAUER.

What is the matter, my child?

MARIE.

Mama, dear, I sat up all night in the train and have had no sleep at all.

[22]

THE FIRES OF ST. JOHN

BRAUER.

And how much longer will it take you ——?

MARIE.

Only one more trip to town, — but pardon me, papa, the new assistant pastor is at the gate and ——

BRAUER.

Who?

MARIE.

The new assistant pastor.

[GERTRUDE *snickers*.]

BRAUER.

[*To* GERTRUDE.]   What are you laughing at?

GERTRUDE.

[*Pulling at* MARIE'S *skirt and can hardly keep from bursting out laughing*.]   I — I — oh, I am not laughing.

BRAUER.

[*To* MARIE.]   But what does he want?

MARIE.

He says he does not wish to disturb the ladies so early in the morning, and asks you to please come out ——

BRAUER.

Nonsense! tell him to come in.

MARIE.

Yes, papa.

GEORGE.

Good-morning, Marie.

MARIE.

Good-morning, George.   [*Exit.*]

BRAUER.

Gertrude, come here. Now remember, my dear, such conduct is not at all becoming to a full-grown young lady.

[23]

GERTRUDE.

My dear, sweet papa, I am so ashamed of myself —
I — I'll never do it again — never. But it's so funny
— ha, ha, ha! he is gone on Marie ——

MRS. BRAUER.

My dear, remember you are now a bride and it would
be far more proper to say ——

GEORGE.

Smitten with her?

MRS. BRAUER.

[*Somewhat reproachfully.*] George!!!

BRAUER.

Sh, sh — silence!

> [*During following scene,* MARIE *noiselessly
> clears off the table.*]

PASTOR.

[*Enters.*] I should not have dared to annoy the
ladies at this early hour, if ——

BRAUER.

[*Laughingly.*] Eight o'clock is not so very early in
the country, my dear Pastor; you will soon learn that
here.

MRS. BRAUER.

And how is the good old pastor?

PASTOR.

[*Doubtfully shrugging his shoulders.*] Well ——!

MRS. BRAUER.

[*Alarmed.*] He is not worse, I hope?

PASTOR.

At the age of eighty, my dear lady, one cannot be
said to be growing stronger.

BRAUER.

Ah, I see, Pastor, you are somewhat of a philosopher. Will you take something?

PASTOR

You are very kind.   A good glass of brandy is half the morning sun.

BRAUER.

Now that is a manly word, Pastor.

PASTOR.

Oh! thank you! Your health!   [*Drinks.*]

BRAUER.

Will you take something, George?

GEORGE.

No thank you, uncle, not now.

MRS. BRAUER

When did you arrive, Pastor?

PASTOR.

Just three weeks ago.

MRS. BRAUER.

And do you like our town?

PASTOR.

Very much indeed, thank you.   I find the whole world beautiful; but the surroundings here are exceptionally so.   Yes, this place to me seems doubly attractive, for here every one seems smiling and happy —— Pardon me, Miss, you have dropped the napkin.

[MARIE *smilingly bows her acknowledgment.*]

[GERTRUDE *exits, stifling a laugh.*]

BRAUER.

Pastor, you will pardon this rudeness, she is still a child.

PASTOR.

Oh, certainly, certainly; for she is right. I have not yet been able to overcome my old tendency to play the gallant in the presence of ladies — and in this frock — I know — I must look somewhat ridiculous.

BRAUER.

Tell me, Pastor, how did you happen to obtain this position?

PASTOR.

Well, you see, that, too, is partly connected with this coat. There were four of us, classmates — who, after graduating, were eagerly awaiting the call to save the sinful world — and among them, myself the only one who was, what you might say, in fairly good financial circumstances. We were now and then compelled, first one and then the other, to present ourselves at the board of directors — and as a consequence my coat suffered severely. Now it really never fitted any one of my comrades and at my suggestion we finally purchased a coat, that came nearer fitting each of us, striking a happy medium, as it were, to every one's satisfaction. Then, about four weeks ago, an ex-fellow-student — the curate of the cathedral — came to us, with this information: " Ye holy men, list ye to me. In yon Lithuanian mountains lives a minister of the gospel, who, on account of his extreme age and feebleness, is incapacitated from properly performing his duties. And as there are four of you, I propose that you draw straws and leave it to chance who shall be the favored one." At that the others unanimously declared: " No, he who has shared with us his clothing shall be the favored one " — and — well, here I am and, I fear, not half as pious as I look.

THE FIRES OF ST. JOHN

BRAUER.

Ah, courage, Pastor, courage ——

PASTOR.

Pray do not think that I am ashamed of my calling; believe me, like our Lord and Master, my heart aches for suffering humanity, and therefore it has ever been my desire to follow in His footsteps. Besides, it was my father's wish. You must know my father is a well-to-do farmer — there are no really large estates in the lowlands — but he has considerable — yes, I might say, a great deal of money — and owing to my early surroundings, I'm afraid I am much better suited for a farmer than a minister of the gospel. But I will not give up, and continue to struggle and rid myself of all my bad habits. Your health!

BRAUER.

Do you know, Pastor, I am beginning to like you! Do you wish to remain here and take the old pastor's place?

PASTOR.

I really would like ——

BRAUER.

Very well, my vote you shall have!

PASTOR.

You are very kind, indeed. With such a position I should be quite content, and to complete my happiness —— but, by-the-bye, the object of my visit was, really, the bridal-sermon. I am afraid our good old pastor will not be able now ——

MRS. BRAUER.

Ah ——

THE FIRES OF ST. JOHN

BRAUER.

[*Simultaneously.*] Will not be equal to the exertion, you mean; ah — I feared as much.

PASTOR.

Therefore, if you will allow me — unless you desired some one else ——

BRAUER.

Pastor, if we had not already heard you in the pulpit I would deny your request, point blank, as you are practically a stranger to us. But your ways and sentiments please me, and therefore — what say you, wife? [*She nods.*] — And you, George?

GEORGE.

Oh, I don't know; but unless I am very much mistaken, there is already a great deal of sympathy between us, eh, Pastor?

PASTOR.

Now I must confess that is rather meaningless, at least so far as I am concerned; for *my* sympathy extends towards the whole world.

GEORGE.

At any rate I am glad ——

PASTOR.

[*Jestingly.*] Then will you kindly leave us for awhile? I desire to inquire into your past record.

GEORGE.

[*Shakes his finger laughingly.*] With pleasure, if you promise not to be too severe on me. [*Exit.*]

PASTOR.

Now, then, with your kind permission, I will take a few notes ——

BRAUER.

Certainly, Pastor!

[28]

THE FIRES OF ST. JOHN

PASTOR.

This young gentleman, your nephew, is especially close to the family, is he not?

BRAUER.

Correct!

PASTOR.

Pardon me, but may I ask in what way?

BRAUER.

I will tell you, Pastor.   It was in the year '67, when we had here in East Prussia, a terrible drought — a year of distress and — do you remember anything about it?

PASTOR.

Very little, as I was then still quite young.

BRAUER.

Ah, it was terrible!   Potatoes and fodder rotted before ripening.   Of wheat and rye hardly a trace.   We farmers, I tell you — !   Then it was, when my brother-in-law, the husband of my sainted sister, whose estates were in the neighboring township yonder, realized one day his financial ruin and with all his aristocratic pride — you understand — he saw no other way — he resorted to the pistol — he committed suicide.

PASTOR.

And the — your sister, still lives?

BRAUER.

Thank God, no! but from that day ——

PASTOR.

Pardon the interruption; but I have heard your daughter, Miss Marie, called " the calamity child " by some of the villagers.   Has that any connection with this year of distress?

[29]

THE FIRES OF ST. JOHN

MRS. BRAUER.

And you didn't know that, Pastor — how she came
into our house? Well, during that same terrible winter,
we were returning one night, my husband and myself,
from the town, where we had at our own expense erected
a soup-kitchen — when suddenly, at the corner of the
woods yonder, where the road makes a sharp turn, our
horses shied — and there, in the middle of the road, we
saw lying, a woman, with a child pressed closely to her
bosom. She refused to stir and begged us to put her
out of her misery. Of course, we took her into the
sleigh at once — ah, she was in an awful condition ——

BRAUER.

I tell you, Pastor, it was months before we could rid
the blankets of vermin.

MRS. BRAUER.

And the child, the poor little thing ——! But after
being bathed and fed, and lying there, between the clean
white covers, we both stood over its bed — the little
thing, with its pinched face, laughed at us and stretched
out its tiny hands — my husband said to me: "Wife, I
believe this is our share of all this sorrow and misery
that heaven has sent us."

BRAUER.

For you must know, Pastor, that our own daughter,
Gertrude, was then not yet born.

MRS. BRAUER.

No, not until three years later. Well, we bought the
child from that miserable, drunken woman, in proper,
legal form — determined and glad to get rid of her, for
she did smell so of gin, I could not endure it any longer.

THE FIRES OF ST. JOHN

BRAUER.

That is what the worst drunkards in these parts prefer to brandy.

PASTOR.

Unfortunately ! ! !

BRAUER.

But to come back to my nephew ——

PASTOR.

Pardon me, another question. What became of the mother?

BRAUER.

Ah, that is a bad story — and just to-day ——

PASTOR.

Yes ——

BRAUER.

Oh — nothing, nothing. Anyway — that woman really did return, and as we did not want the child to see her, we gave her more money. Of course she remembered that and so finally she became a positive plague.

MRS. BRAUER.

Oh, Henry, I have often thought since, perhaps a mother's heart prompted her ——

BRAUER.

You think so, eh? Then perhaps a mother's heart also prompted her to steal at the same time! for every time she honored us with a visit, something or other disappeared, until I grew suspicious, had her watched, she was caught red-handed — and, of course, a long term in prison was the result.

PASTOR.

And the girl — does she know or suspect anything at all?

THE FIRES OF ST. JOHN

MRS. BRAUER.

We told her, her mother was dead. But one day she really did see her.

PASTOR.

How did that misfortune happen?

MRS. BRAUER.

It was on her confirmation day, just as the girls left the church in a body, when we heard a cry. What had happened? Why, that woman had been lying in wait for the procession; when suddenly she appeared, seized her child, and kneeling before her in the road, passionately covered her hands and feet with kisses.

PASTOR.

[*Shuddering*.] Horrible! ! ! ! ! !

MRS. BRAUER.

I tore the child from her arms, of course, and carried her into the house. We had to make some kind of an explanation; a drunken vagabond, I told her! Did she believe it? — H'm? — Then she fell ill——

PASTOR.

And how is it now?

BRAUER.

[*Humorously*.] Why, Pastor, you seem very much interested.

GEORGE.

[*Enters*. GERTRUDE *follows him in*.] I presume I am pretty well done by this time.

BRAUER.

We haven't even started with your case. The pastor is interested in something of far greater importance.

THE FIRES OF ST. JOHN

PASTOR.

[*With meaning and moved.*]   You must not believe that, Mr. von Harten;. but there are lives whose fates are surrounded by so much mystery —— [*with a glance at* MARIE, *who enters L. with package of linen.*]

GEORGE.

[*Who follows his glance.*]   Yes, yes, you are right.

PASTOR.

If you will allow me, I will call again about the sermon.

MRS. BRAUER.

[*Giving him her hand.*]   Pastor, you know you are always welcome in this house.

BRAUER.

Give my regards to our good old pastor.   Towards evening we will see him, as usual.

PASTOR.

Oh, I had almost forgotten! He desires me to ask you kindly, should you again favor him with eggnog, to please add a little more sugar, for the last was a trifle tart.

MRS. BRAUER.

Why, of course, the poor old soul.

PASTOR.

Do not say that, madame; for when the time has come when all our wishes and hopes and desires are concentrated upon a small quantity of sweets, our sufferings are near the end.   And now, adieu.   Miss Marie, adieu.

MARIE.

[*Preoccupied.*]   Adieu.

[PASTOR *exits, accompanied by* BRAUER.]
[GERTRUDE *enters.*]

[33]

MRS. BRAUER.

Don't be afraid dear, no one will scold you.

GERTRUDE.

Oh mama, I'm so ashamed of myself. When he arrived he seemed so jolly — and now — I am sure he is offended.

GEORGE.

He was not offended, dear, only a little grave.

MRS. BRAUER.

At any rate, what do you think of him, Marie?

MARIE.

[*Glancing up from her work, sorting linen.*] Of whom, mama dear?

MRS. BRAUER.

Why, the new pastor.

MARIE.

Oh mama, my mind is so occupied, I hadn't given him a thought.

GERTRUDE.

[*Aside to* GEORGE.] Now you tell her, George.

MARIE.

Gertrude, how about our manzanillo-tree — any blossoms this morning?

MRS. BRAUER.

You don't mean to say you haven't looked after that beloved tree of yours this morning?

MARIE.

I have had no time, mama dear.

GERTRUDE.

[*To* GEORGE.] Now tell her.

GEORGE.

Marie, both Gertrude and myself insist, that you cease this endless drudgery for our sakes; it isn't right.

[MARIE, *humming, pays no heed — looks into space.*]

GERTRUDE.

See, she is not even listening.

MRS. BRAUER.

What's that you are singing?

MARIE.

I — ? Was I singing?

MRS. BRAUER.

Well then, humming.

MARIE.

Oh yes, last night at the station I heard a strange song — some one in a fourth-class coach was singing Listen. [*Sings.*]

" Zwirio czcnay, zwirio tenay — kam'mano bernyczo —
Rid wid wil dai dai — Ne'r mano bernyczo."

GEORGE.

And the Lithuanian text — you memorized it just from hearing it?

MARIE.

Certainly.

GEORGE.

Well, where did you learn all that?

MARIE.

Why, I have always known it.

GEORGE.

And could you translate it readily?

MARIE.

Oh, it means nothing, really — [*makes one or two attempts.*]—" here " — no !
" I look here and I look there — where may be my lover?
Rid wid will dai dai — Nowhere is my lover ! "

BRAUER.

[*Enters during this, unseen by her, puts arms around her. She shrieks.*] There, there — [*caressing her.*] Patience, my darling, some day you will have one — perhaps very soon.   Why, what's the matter, dear?

MARIE.

[*Leans on him in tearless sobbing.*]   Oh, you have frightened me so !

BRAUER.

What is the matter with you this morning?   What has happened?

MARIE.

I have already told you, nothing.

BRAUER.

Tut, tut! something has gone wrong! I can see it — and now, I demand that you tell me the truth.

MARIE.

Well, then — yes !

BRAUER.

What is it?   Come, come, out with it.

MARIE.

Some one attacked me.

BRAUER.

Attacked you?

MARIE.

Not far from here.

BRAUER.

As you came from the station?

MARIE.

Yes.

BRAUER.

Well, I never — but every one around here knows you and your character; how did he look? was it a vaga-bond?

MARIE.

[*Hesitatingly.*] N—No. It was—a gentleman——

BRAUER.

Did he lay hands on you, or even try to touch you?

MARIE.

No.

BRAUER.

But you say he attacked you?

MARIE.

Attacked me — yes!

BRAUER.

You mean he followed you?

MARIE.

Yes.

BRAUER

How far?

MARIE.

As far as the gate, which I opened quickly and then he disappeared.

BRAUER.

[*To the others.*] Now, what do you say to that? [GEORGE *shrugs his shoulders.*] There is something queer about it all. [*To* MARIE.] And that is what upset you so?

MARIE.

Oh, I am already much composed.

BRAUER.

[*Raises her head.*]   Yes — you look it.

GERTRUDE.

Oh, papa, don't torment her so.

BRAUER.

Now, then, go and take a good nap.

MARIE.

Not yet, papa dear, I can't.   I must speak with George first.   About the large bookcase — I really don't know where to place it.

BRAUER.

But you can do that later, can't you?

MARIE.

I fear I might forget it.

BRAUER.

Very well; I am going down to look after the cow. Will you come, wife?

MRS. BRAUER.

[*Rising and putting up her handwork.*]   Yes, dear.

BRAUER.

[*To* MARIE.]   And one thing more,—don't you put your foot outside of the gate without an escort hereafter!   Understand?   Not once!

MARIE.

But why not, papa dear?

BRAUER.

After what has happened?   But I never heard of such a thing — never, as long as I ——

MRS. BRAUER.

But, Henry, in broad daylight, it is hardly necessary ——

BRAUER.

No matter; I have my reasons for that; besides —
well, I'll tell you later.

MRS. BRAUER.

[*In passing taps* MARIE *on cheek*.]   Now, pet, go and
take a good rest.   [*Both exit.*]

MARIE.

You must go, too, Gertrude!

GERTRUDE.

[*Peevishly*.]   But why should I?

MARIE.

You know, dear, your future home ——

GERTRUDE.

Ah, yes; those stupid furnishings!   Do you know,
I don't think a wedding half so much fun as Christmas.
Now don't be long, will you?   [*Exit.*]
                                                [*Pause.*]

GEORGE.

Why so deep in thought, suddenly?

MARIE.

I — ?   Oh, I was thinking.   I was picturing to myself
that cosy little nook, your corner room!

GEORGE.

Marie, dear, how can I ever thank you for all the ——

MARIE.

Don't speak of it, George, for I take great delight in
having the furniture moved about; and then, I say to
myself: "Here is where they will take their tea, and
there they will while away their leisure hours" — so ——
But, what I meant to tell you!   Yesterday we had an
accident — the large mirror in the parlor was broken.
I know it portends ill ——

GEORGE.

What care I, so long as our friendship will not be broken.

MARIE.

But why should it?

GEORGE.

It shall never be my fault, Marie.

MARIE.

Certainly never mine. But what I wanted to say,—I had the large mahogany bookcase repolished. Is that satisfactory?

GEORGE.

Anything you choose to do is satisfactory to me.

MARIE.

[*Hesitatingly.*] And then—I must tell you, George, something important. When I unpacked the bookcase, I found a blue manuscript.

GEORGE.

[*Unsuspecting.*] What kind of a manuscript?

MARIE.

George, you must not leave that lying around—not even hidden behind the books, especially now, when you take your wife to your home.

GEORGE.

In heaven's name, what manuscript?

MARIE.

I believe—it contains some poems——

GEORGE.

You believe—it contains some poems. I have missed it since early last winter; I thought I had lost it. Marie, now tell me truthfully, have you read its contents?

M A R I E .

N — no !

G E O R G E .

Then why do you tell me not to leave it around?

M A R I E .

Well, I read the first part, and had begun on the second, when I concluded to go no further.

G E O R G E .

And you really looked no further than the first? Absolutely no further?

M A R I E .

No.

G E O R G E .

Can you swear to that?

M A R I E .

I can !

G E O R G E .

Then swear !

M A R I E .

I swear ! Are you satisfied?

G E O R G E .

Yes, thank heaven ! But you must not imagine for a moment that the book contains anything I am ashamed of ; on the contrary, I consider it so sacred I would not have it desecrated by a stranger's eye. About four years ago, something occurred within me — within my soul. No one knows — no one could even guess, and no one shall ever know.

M A R I E .

No one? Not even I?

G E O R G E .

No, not even you. But where is the book? Give it to me !

THE FIRES OF ST. JOHN

MARIE.

[*Turns up stage and takes it from her bosom.*] Here it is.

GEORGE.

How shall I ever thank you?

MARIE.

I want you to do me one favor. Will you promise me?

GEORGE.

If it's in my power, certainly!

MARIE.

Then I must first confess to you. A few moments ago, when papa questioned me, I deceived him. I was attacked last night — yes — but not by a man, but by a woman — a Lithuanian woman. George, that woman was my mother!

GEORGE.

But I understood your mother was dead.

MARIE.

No, no; that is not so. Not one of you ever told me the truth. On the day of my confirmation I was waylaid by that very same woman — I cannot have been mistaken.

GEORGE.

Come, tell me, how did it happen?

MARIE.

I was walking along quietly — 'twas already dawning — when suddenly a gaunt form arose from the ditch beside the road. I looked, and saw before me a miserable beggarwoman, who called out to me in a trembling voice: "Marie — Madame — Daughter!" I turned cold in fear and horror, and, unable to utter one sound, I began to run; and I ran, ran, ran, and behind me I only heard her agonizing call: "My Marie — my daughter!" And so, I ran away from my own mother. And now, after a few hours' thought, I realize I did wrong. I must see her and speak to her, and learn from her own lips who and what I am; and as papa has forbidden me to leave this house — I would go in spite of him, but I have a fear — I beg of you, George, dear, go to her, I implore you, find her for me — she cannot be far away, and ——

GEORGE.

And then ——?

MARIE.

Then bring her to me, into the garden, or, better still, into this room towards evening, when papa and mama are calling on the old pastor ——

GEORGE.

Marie, I cannot do that!

MARIE.

The first time I ask a favor of you — and you say you cannot do it?

GEORGE.

Marie, dear, listen to me! You have been so kind to me of late — and that has not always been so; but if you had sacrificed for me even more than your own comfort and rest, I — I could not do it — I could not deceive your father and mother, for I fear the consequences.

MARIE.

Then can't you understand that, a foundling though I am, a desire might come over me to see my own mother, though she be but a common beggar and an outcast? That I might want to lay my head on her shoulder and be petted and fondled, and cry myself to sleep on mine — on my own mother's breast?

GEORGE.

Are you not fondled, are you not petted — has mama not always been kind to you?

MARIE.

Yes, but it is not the same — not the same. Never have I felt the desire, the demand within me for my own flesh and blood, as just now.

GEORGE.

But why just now?

MARIE.

[*Imploringly*.] Because my heart is bursting. Oh, George!

GEORGE.

I cannot. I dare not do it!

MARIE.

Then you refuse me?

GEORGE.

You know I must!!

MARIE.

Then have you forgotten what took place in there, in your heart, four years ago?

[*Pause*.]

GEORGE.

Marie, you have read my manuscript!

MARIE.

Yes, I read it. Will you do it now?

GEORGE.

Marie, you have sworn falsely!!!

THE FIRES OF ST. JOHN

MARIE.

[*Shrugging her shoulders*.]   Will you do as I ask?

GEORGE.

'Tis well!   I will do as you ask!!!!

[*Curtain*.]

END OF THE FIRST ACT.

ACT TWO

The same scene as Act I.

[MARIE, *seated, with some linen in her lap, at the sewing-machine, looking dreamily out of the window*.]

HOUSEKEEPER KATIE.

[*In door R.*]

May I come in, Miss Marie?

MARIE.

Oh, is that you? Yes, come in!

KATIE.

I see you are working on Miss Gertrude's wedding outfit. How beautiful, fit for a princess. But what I wanted to ask you: Madame has given me the menu for the wedding feast, and as to fish, it calls for carp. Now you know I am economical, but carp — common carp ——

MARIE.

Why, carp is a very fine fish ——

KATIE.

Oh yes, and good enough for — say — your wedding feast; but not good enough for Miss Gertrude.

MARIE.

For my wedding feast even carp is too good.

[46]

THE FIRES OF ST. JOHN

Oh no; carp is not too good for you, though it may be good enough — and do you know I will prepare a special Polish sauce — but Miss Gertrude — she must have deep sea fish. Now will you see Madame about that, please?

MARIE.

Very well, I will speak to mama about it.

KATIE.

And you are not offended?

MARIE.

Oh no!

KATIE.

For, after all, you know, you are only a foundling.

MARIE.

Oh yes, I know.

KATIE.

But we all love you, Miss Marie, and ——

MARIE.

Thank you. But have you seen Mr. von Harten this morning?

KATIE.

No, I have not! But I have some good news for you — the assistant pastor has fallen deeply in love with you.

MARIE.

Yes?

KATIE.

And he is going to ask for your hand!!! I always said you were a lucky girl. Just think, you may be a St. John's-bride.

MARIE.

And what is a St. John's-bride?

THE FIRES OF ST. JOHN

KATIE.

You don't know that, Miss Marie? Well, I'll tell you. It is written in the new seal of Solomonis: "Whoever shall give or receive their first kiss on St. John's eve, their love is sealed and they will be faithful unto death." So it is written in the new seal of Solomonis.

GERTRUDE.

[*Enter C., hands behind her, with bouquet.*]

Marie, I have something for you. No, first I want Katie to leave the room. Go now, go!!!

KATIE.

Oh, I am going—I am going!!!!!!!!! [*Exit.*]

GERTRUDE.

Shut your eyes now! [MARIE *does so, as* GERTRUDE *holds bouquet to* MARIE'S *face.*] Now what is it?

MARIE.

The tulip-tree! the first blossoms from our manzanillo-tree! It blooms—it blooms!!! [*Burying her face in the flowers.*]

GERTRUDE.

Are you glad, Marie?

MARIE.

Yes, darling, so glad!!! Thank you!

GERTRUDE.

And do you know who picked them?—George!

MARIE.

For me?

GERTRUDE.

Why, of course, for you!

MARIE.

He—did this—for me?

[48]

GERTRUDE.

He would do even more than that for me, I am sure!

MARIE.

Oh yes, certainly! But where is he now?

GERTRUDE.

I don't know!

MARIE.

Did he say he had to go somewhere?

GERTRUDE.

Yes, he had to go out on the fields, he said — and that was quite some time ago. I wanted to accompany him, I begged and begged, but he flatly refused to let me go.

MARIE.

[*Breathing heavily.*] Oh!!!!!!!!

GERTRUDE.

I don't know how it is; but to-day he is acting so strangely. Papa has asked for him several times — and do you know, dear, at times he is not at all pleasant to me!

MARIE.

But why should he ——

GERTRUDE.

That's just it! why should he? Oh, if I only knew — if I was only certain he loved me — and then, another thing — I don't know if I should tell you — I have a growing fear, some other girl will take him away from me.

MARIE.

[*With forced laugh.*] Away from you, dear? how could that be possible?

THE FIRES OF ST. JOHN

GERTRUDE.

Oh yes, you may laugh; but at times, when he looks at me, I see a strange look come in his eyes. Half affection — half pity — and I don't want to be pitied! Why should he? Am I not happy?

MARIE.

[*Caressing her.*] Yes, dear; you ought to be very, very happy.

GERTRUDE.

But I cannot rid myself of the fear, perhaps he really loves another and is only taking compassion on me! Oh, if I only knew ——

MARIE.

But, my darling ——

GERTRUDE.

For you see, I am still so young — and think, how ill-mannered I was only this morning! I was so sorry afterwards — but I do love to laugh. [*Laughs.*]

MARIE.

[*With strange, desperate tone of voice.*] And you shall laugh — laugh — laugh — so — so —— !!!!!!!

GERTRUDE.

Mama, too, insists that my love for him is only that of a child and not of a woman and a bride; but you see she would rather I'd not marry at all and so remain at home with her all my life. But you will be good to her, won't you? You will soon be her only one.

MARIE.

I —— ?

GERTRUDE.

Why yes!

THE FIRES OF ST. JOHN

MARIE.

I shall soon know whose only one I am!

GERTRUDE.

What are you saying?

MARIE.

[*As* GEORGE *enters.*]   There he is!

[GERTRUDE *runs towards him.*   MARIE *takes
a few steps, then hesitates and stops.*]

GERTRUDE.

[*Pulling him, as she runs towards him.*]   Oh,
George!!! [*Then*]   Confound you ——!

GEORGE.

[*Reproachfully.*]   *Gertrude!!!!!!*

GERTRUDE.

[*Crushed.*]   Why, what did I say?

GEORGE.

[*Lovingly.*]   Now listen to me, little one.   Such language may be excusable in your papa, but never in my bride.

GERTRUDE.

[*Pouting.*]   Everything I say seems to displease you. You never find fault with Marie!   You can go and marry her!!!

GEORGE.

Marie does not want to marry me.

MARIE.

My very best thanks, George!

GEORGE.

For what?

MARIE.

[*Picking up bouquet.*]   For this!

[51]

GEORGE.

Oh, don't mention it.

MARIE.

Were you out in the fields?

GEORGE.

Yes.

GERTRUDE.

Yes, papa is angry with you, too.   He is looking for you!

GEORGE.

Oh yes — I know —— ! Well?

MARIE.

In what direction did you go?

GEORGE.

I have been everywhere.

MARIE.

And have you found —— ?

GERTRUDE.

What was he to find?

GEORGE.

Yes, what was I to find?—— But, children, your tulip-tree is certainly a strange fellow. There he stands, blooming alone, like the last rose of summer ——

GERTRUDE.

My great-grandfather brought it from South America!

GEORGE.

[*To* MARIE.]   And that is why you love it so, because it is so foreign and strange?

MARIE.

[*Busy with linen.*]   Perhaps!

GERTRUDE.

No, that is not the reason ——

MARIE.

Well then, what is it?

GERTRUDE.

I'm going to tell on you.   One day papa took her to
the Opera, down in the city; there they saw the
African ——

GEORGE.

" L'Africaine," you mean?

GERTRUDE.

Yes, yes, that's what she called it.

MARIE.

Gertrude, please don't ——

GERTRUDE.

In that play occurs a poison-tree — I think ——

GEORGE.

Yes, a manzanillo-tree !

GERTRUDE.

Yes, yes; and whosoever inhales the odor of its blossoms must die.   And do you know what she did?   Oh,
yes, I did the same — we would go to this tree, smell of
its blossoms, and lay down ——

GEORGE.

To die?

GERTRUDE.

To die.

MARIE.

Now you can imagine, George, how long ago that
must have been.

GERTRUDE.

Yes, it was long, long ago.   But about four years
ago, one day Marie really wanted to die very badly.

[*Marie casts a frightened glance at* GEORGE,
who returns it thoughtfully.]

[53]

GERTRUDE.

But we didn't.

GEORGE.

No, no, thank heaven. Now, little one, run along and tell papa that I am here.

GERTRUDE.

Marie, will you come, too?

MARIE.

No; I think I will remain here a little while longer.

GERTRUDE.

Then I'll stay, too.

GEORGE.

Now, little one ——

[GERTRUDE *exits with a sigh.*]

MARIE.

[*Quickly and suppressed.*] Did you find her? [GEORGE *nods.*] Will she come? Why don't you answer?

GEORGE.

Marie, when you exacted this promise from me this morning, I did not realize what it meant. I had never seen your — I don't want to speak that word — I had never seen this person until to-day. She must not come to this house, secretly — she must not!!!

MARIE.

George!!!

GEORGE.

Take uncle into your confidence, at least.

MARIE.

No, no one — no one but you!!

GEORGE.

What do you want with her? You know you belong
to this house. Here you have everything your heart
desires. Here you have love — here you have ——

MARIE.

[*Interrupts him.*] Bread! Why don't you say it?
Yes, here I have bread!

GEORGE

I did not mean to say that.

MARIE.

No; but I did! And do I not earn it, as well as the
little love I obtain in this house? I am " The Calamity
Child " — and I do not ask for charity.

GEORGE.

You seem to be possessed of the very devil to-day!

MARIE.

Perhaps!

GEORGE.

I implore you, do not insist. I fear the consequence.
You will see! for whatever is done against nature,
punishes itself.

MARIE.

And is it against nature when a child cries out for its
own mother?

GEORGE.

She is not your mother; your mother is in this house.

MARIE.

Gertrude's mother is in this house, not mine. A
mother must feel for her child, she must see ——

GEORGE.

Sh — sh!

[*Enter* GERTRUDE.]

GERTRUDE.

You two are continually talking in whispers; can't you tell *me?* It makes me so unhappy!

MARIE.

[*Caressing her.*] But darling, it is all done for your sake!

> [*During this*, GEORGE *looks at her disapprovingly, while* MARIE *casts a timid glance at him.*]

BRAUER.

[*Enters.*] At last you have come. Where in thunder have you been all day? It almost seemed to me as if you were trying to avoid me!

GEORGE.

But, uncle ——

BRAUER.

Well, girls, have you prepared the pastor's eggnog?

MARIE.

Oh, I had entirely forgotten it.

BRAUER.

Then see to it at once. And don't forget the sugar, you know.

MARIE.

Yes, papa.

BRAUER.

And Gertrude dear, you can go and help her. It is time you were learning to do something yourself.

GERTRUDE.

Yes, papa!

MARIE.

I hardly think it will be ready in time to take with you and mama.

BRAUER.

Then bring it later — yourself.

MARIE.

[*With a glance at* GEORGE.]   Could not Gertrude bring it, papa?   I have so much work to do!

GERTRUDE.

No, no, papa!!!

BRAUER.

Yes, yes, you shall! — bring it up when done; and mind, you remain at the pastor's as long as your mother and I, this time.   Understand?

GERTRUDE.

Oh, papa dear!   The last time, the old pastor insisted upon holding my hand in his so long; and they are so cold and clammy, so shriveled and hairy, like the hands of the dead!

BRAUER.

Come here, my child.   Those hairy hands once christened you, and at your confirmation the same shriveled hands were laid upon your head and invoked for you the blessings of heaven; and would you, after all that, refuse to hold them in your own warm young hands?   My daughter, I do not wish to hear that again.   [*Kisses her.*]

MARIE.

[*Slowly has approached* GEORGE.   *Softly, aside to him.*]   You will do as I ask?

BRAUER.

And now, leave us.

[MARIE *and* GERTRUDE *exit.*]

"Now, then, comes your turn," says the stork to the worm.

THE FIRES OF ST. JOHN

GEORGE.

[*Looking after the girls, turns.*] I suppose so, but take a care, uncle, I am not so easily digested.

BRAUER.

We shall see! We shall see!

GEORGE.

What do you want with me? My financial condition is satisfactory. I have a good position, and my future is assured. I desire to enjoy the results of my *own* labors, not those of yours.

BRAUER.

So, so!

GEORGE.

Yes, dear uncle. If you were so determined upon giving a large dowry, you should have found another husband for Gertrude than myself.

BRAUER.

[*Riled.*] Oh, hang you and your confounded pride!

GEORGE.

Yes, I am proud; and because of my pride and determination, and, I may say, defiance, I have become what I am!

BRAUER.

[*Rather arrogantly.*] And was there no diligence?

GEORGE.

That, also, was nothing but defiance.

BRAUER.

I almost believe you are determined to create another rumpus, as you did twelve years ago.

GEORGE.

If necessary, yes!

[58]

BRAUER.

And was it necessary, even then?

GEORGE.

You ask me that question? When one day I came here, during vacation from college, you insisted upon my attending your church. I refused. You gave me my choice, either to do as you asked, or have my allowance cut off. Then I resolved in my mind never to comply with your command, in spite of everything. Oh, it is no pleasure to hunger, as I was forced to do then; but you may believe me, as I stand before you now, a free and independent man, I owe all of it to my stubborn confidence in myself, looking neither to right nor left, but straight ahead, without concessions, without falsehoods, always able to look every man straight in the face. And this good conscience is my proudest possession. From it do I draw all my strength, and I will never give it up.

BRAUER.

Well, who the devil asked you to give it up?

GEORGE.

And one thing more. Of course, I belong to this house; fate has made it my lot. Therefore it has ever been far from my mind to seek a wife elsewhere, so strongly attached do I feel myself to this house; and that would have been impossible, had I not from that day been a free man. And now, dear uncle, you are at heart a good and kind man; but your hand is heavy, and it must not lie upon me again as that of the master. For that reason do I refuse to touch even one penny of the dowry, now or any other time.

BRAUER.

So, so! Then you are really afraid of me?

GEORGE.

Afraid of you? Bah!!!

BRAUER.

And at heart you are nothing but a coward!!

GEORGE.

Uncle, I forbid you ——

BRAUER.

You forbid me? Ha! This is my house, and here I am the master!

[GEORGE *shrugs his shoulders.*]

BRAUER.

Yes, yes; it seems to annoy you to have any one keep an eye on you and your conduct ——

GEORGE.

My life has been as an open book to this day.

BRAUER.

But after to-day — what about that? Who can look into the future? Who can look into your heart and read your thoughts? Who knows what may happen over night, eh?

GEORGE.

Uncle, these are insults I will not endure, even from you ——

BRAUER.

Well! What then! Come on! [*Jumps up, facing him, ready to fight.*]

MRS. BRAUER.

[*Enters, ready to go out, dressed.*] Henry, what on earth have you done to Gertrude? She is in her room, crying as if her heart would break.

[MARIE *has also come in with* MRS. BRAUER.]

THE FIRES OF ST. JOHN

BRAUER.

How is the eggnog getting on, Marie?

MARIE.

It is not quite done, papa!

BRAUER.

Then let her have her cry; she can bring it up later.

MARIE.

Yes, papa.

MRS. BRAUER.

And are you ready?

BRAUER.

Ready for what?

MRS. BRAUER.

Are you ready to go now?

BRAUER.

Well, wait for me out on the veranda; we have something to settle first, we two!

MRS. BRAUER.

What's the matter with George?

BRAUER.

Oh, I have just asked him for an explanation, and that does not seem to please him.

MRS. BRAUER.

[*Caressing him.*]   Don't you mind him, George dear. After the wedding you can laugh at him.

BRAUER.

Well, we shall see about that ! ! !

[MRS. BRAUER *and* MARIE *exit.*]

BRAUER.

We can't go on like this, for I fear the consequences; but, nevertheless, I shall handle you without gloves.

[61]

THE FIRES OF ST. JOHN

GEORGE.

Well?

BRAUER.

My child loves you. You are her ideal, her all, and the wedding must take place. But tell me, what right have you to all this pride — I might even say arrogance?

GEORGE.

Must I perhaps ask your permission ——— ?

BRAUER.

That is the same old defiance, the same unreasonable stubbornness of your father's ——— ! ! ! ! !

GEORGE.

[*Starts.*] My father has been dead these twenty years — what do you want of him now?

BRAUER.

What do I want of him? That he left you to me, to bring up from childhood, I will hardly mention; although that ought to be sufficient to temper your untamable pride — at least towards me; but ———

GEORGE.

Uncle, you may abuse me as much as you please, but my father I will not have disturbed! My father — you shall let him rest in peace!

BRAUER.

And who was it — who took care — who made it possible, that he could rest in peace?

GEORGE.

Uncle, what do you mean?

BRAUER.

Well then, who was it, when he laid there, dead, before us, who paid his debts of honor and saved your father's name from disgrace? [*Pause.*]

[62]

THE FIRES OF ST. JOHN

GEORGE.

Uncle, you should not have said that!

[*Sinks in chair and covers his face with his hands.*]

BRAUER.

My boy —— [*Emotion stops him from saying more — walks about.*]   See here —— [*Again the same — tries to light a cigar, breaks it and throws it away.*]

GEORGE.

You should not have said that, uncle!   No, no ——

BRAUER.

My God, you knew of it?

GEORGE.

Yes, I knew of it, and yet you should not have said it; you should not have repeated it.   Twelve years ago, in our quarrel, when you raised your whip to me — and I reached for the carving-knife — no, no — I should not have done *that*.   You should not have raised your whip, nor I the knife.   That is the reason I refused anything from you at all.   Now you know it.   From that day I swore to scratch the gold from the ground with my finger nails and fling it in your face.   From that day I hated you — and rightly so!

BRAUER.

And all that because I saved your and your father's name from dishonor and disgrace?

GEORGE.

No!   But because you turned that same deed into a weapon to crush my youthful pride.

BRAUER.

My boy, one uses the weapon nearest to hand.

THE FIRES OF ST. JOHN

GEORGE.

[*Bitterly.*] Even if it is only a whip. But then, I see my mistake. I have no right to pride; my fatherly inheritance does not permit it. Give me your gold! I'll take it! All — all ——!

BRAUER.

No, no; in your present state of mind I will force nothing on you. You might again turn to hating me.

GEORGE.

Ah no, dear uncle, that is past. Hereafter, I will swallow my pride.

BRAUER.

My boy ——

MARIE.

[*Enters.*] Pardon me papa, but mama asks, if you are not yet ready to go?

BRAUER.

[*With a glance at* GEORGE.] Well, as far as I am concerned, I am ready now! [*Takes his hat.*] Marie, give him a glass of brandy to brace [him up. [*Goes to door and returns.*]. George?

GEORGE.

Uncle? [BRAUER *offers his hand.*] My hand I cannot refuse you.

BRAUER.

[*Goes to door. In door.*] Yes, and your heart, too, I will win again — or I'll be damned!!!!

[*Exits, slamming door.*]

MARIE.

What did he say to you, George?

GEORGE.

Do not ask me, do not ask me! [*Walks about.*] All these years I have struggled and deprived myself with only one thing in view — to be free — free — and yet I must bow — I must bow. If it were not for the sake of this beautiful child, who is innocent of it all, I would be tempted to —— But the die is cast, the yoke is ready — and so am I!!!!!!!!

MARIE.

[*Softly and hesitating.*] But, George, dear, here in this house, I see nothing for you but love — the yoke seems so light ——

GEORGE.

How pious and tame you have suddenly become!

MARIE.

I am not pious.

GEORGE.

What was that you said a few moments ago? "I am the calamity child. I am the child of misery; but I do not ask for charity." That is what you said of yourself, and it is also true of me. I, *too*, am a child of misery, a calamity child; but I *am* a subject of charity. I accept all they have to give — all — all — ha, ha, ha —— !

MARIE.

You, George, a calamity child?

GEORGE.

Yes! Was I not picked up from the street, as my uncle so kindly informed me for the second time — like yourself? Do I not belong to this house, and am I not smothered with the damnable charity of my benefactors, like yourself?

[65]

MARIE.

I receive my share with thanks.

GEORGE.

And you enjoy serving ——

MARIE.

I enjoy serving!!

GEORGE.

But I — I wish to rule — to command!!!

MARIE.

And you shall rule — you shall command ——

GEORGE.

[*Walking about and ironically.*] Ah yes!!!

MARIE.

[*Timidly.*] George?

GEORGE.

Well?

MARIE.

[*The same.*] Pardon me; but have you forgotten —?

GEORGE.

Oh, I see!

MARIE.

I know it is wrong in me to annoy you at this time, when you are so occupied with affairs of your own —— Besides, you have already refused me once ——

GEORGE.

Wha — yes, now in spite of them all, I am my own master. I am responsible to no one. I have promised you — I shall keep my word!!!!!

MARIE.

Thank you, George!

GEORGE.

Oh, don't thank me ——

MARIE.

Where is she now?

GEORGE.

She is waiting, behind yonder garden hedge.

MARIE.

My God! Do not keep her waiting any longer; call her in here.

GEORGE.

Gertrude is still in the house.

MARIE.

I will get her out of the way. When I appear out there on the veranda, the coast is clear!!

GEORGE.

Marie, for your own sake, I warn you for the last time; discovery means certain disaster.

MARIE.

One disaster more or less, it matters little!

GEORGE.

Is that your last word? Very well, I will bring her to you. [*Gets his hat and goes out centre door.*]

MARIE.

[*Opens door L. and calls out.*] Gertrude! Gertrude!
[*A door is heard to open.*]

GERTRUDE.

[*Outside, with crying voice.*] What is it?

MARIE.

Come quickly, or papa will be angry!

GERTRUDE.

[*After a moment's pause.*] I am coming! [*Another short pause and she appears in door.*]

MARIE.

How red your eyes are! You have been crying!
What's the matter, dear? [*Caressing her.*]

GERTRUDE.

Where is George?

MARIE.

[*Lightly.*] He went out again a few moments ago.

GERTRUDE.

And he didn't ask to see me?

MARIE.

He heard you were crying and did not want to disturb you.

GERTRUDE.

But, Marie, what is the matter with your own eyes?
And you look so queerly ——

MARIE.

My pet, they are the eyes that God has given me
and ——

GERTRUDE.

[*Suspiciously.*] What?

[*A knock at door is heard.*]

MARIE.

Come in!

MAID SERVANT.

[*Enters with basket.*] Here are the eggnog and cakes,
for the pastor. Now be careful and don't crush them!

MARIE.

Very well!

[*Exit* SERVANT.]

GERTRUDE.

[*Taking basket.*] Good-bye, Marie!

[68]

MARIE.

Good-bye, Gertie dear!

[GERTRUDE *starts towards centre door.*]

MARIE.

[*Frightened.*]   Where are you going?

GERTRUDE.

I am going through the garden across the fields; perhaps I will meet George.

MARIE.

[*Concerned.*]   No, no; you must not walk across the fields alone.   Papa has forbidden it.

GERTRUDE.

But I may meet George.

MARIE.

But if you shouldn't, what then?   No, no, I will not allow it!   I will not!   I had such a fright last night.

GERTRUDE.

[*Goes up to the other door and turns back once more.*] Marie, you are not angry with me?

MARIE.

[*Embracing her.*]   My darling!!!

GERTRUDE.

Then I will go that way!   [*Looks all around.*]   Give my love to George!

MARIE.

But I won't see him, dear ——

GERTRUDE.

Well, perhaps you may!

MARIE.

In that case, I will tell him ——

THE FIRES OF ST. JOHN

GERTRUDE.

Very well.

[*Exit R.*]

[MARIE *goes out on veranda — gives sign — returns — locks doors R. and L. — then at C. door — in terror, with searching eyes, she slowly retreats backwards, her eyes glued on the outer darkness — until she finally covers her face with her hands, and is standing against the wall.*]

GEORGE.

[*Enters.*] Here she is!!

GYPSY.

[*Enters.* GEORGE *goes out on veranda, looking off.*] Mine lady, mine daughter — yes — don't be afraid. Oh, you are such a fine lady — you have lover — **you** marry, they say ——?

MARIE.

[*Forcing herself to speak.*] No; I'm not to be married! It is Gertrude, my foster sister.

GYPSY.

You no marry, eh? Never mind — you marry some day — some day [*Examining* MARIE'S *dress with her fingers.*] What a fine dress you have, and all wool —— [*Same with apron.*] Oh, and a silk apron — all silk! Give me, give me?

[MARIE *takes it off and gives it to her.*]

GYPSY.

Thank you — thank you!!! [*Kisses* MARIE'S *sleeve and dress, but when she would kiss her hand,* MARIE *withdraws it quickly.*]

[70]

MARIE.

No, no! *Ne dosu ranka!*

GYPSY.

All right, all right! You are fine lady. [*Looks about.*] Is the old man home, eh?

MARIE.

No, he is out.

GYPSY.

That is good, that is good! He is an old devil — is the old man! All Prussians are devils. But he have fine house, he have! Like a prince!!! [*Rubs her hand over table cover.*] Ah, nice shawl that would make —— [*Sees linen.*] And what fine linen — [*Motions to* MARIE.] Come here!

MARIE.

[*Approaching her.*] What do you want?

GYPSY.

[*Pointing with thumb.*] Give me an drink — just an little drink! [*Indicates with finger and thumb.*]

> [*While* MARIE *turns to sideboard, she quickly takes two or three pieces of linen and with left hand holds them hidden under her apron.*]

GYPSY.

[*After taking drink from* MARIE.] Thanks, mine daughter, thanks! [*After drinking, rubs her stomach.*] Ah, that's good, that's good! — Give me another! [MARIE *fills another glass for her — she drinks it.*] Thank you, thank you!! But now I must be going!

> [*In her anxiety to get out she drops one piece, while going to the door.*]

MARIE.

[*Horrified.*] Mo — mo — what were you trying to do?

GYPSY.

[*Pretending surprise.*]   My, my — just see!   I found this out on the field.   [*Picks it up and puts it under her arm.*]

MARIE.

Put that down, it is not yours.

GYPSY.

[*Doing so.*]   All right, all right — my — my — my ——

MARIE.

Put down all you have!

GYPSY.

I have no more, no, no more, I swear!

MARIE.

[*Goes quickly to door and calls.*]   George!

GEORGE.

[*Enters.*]   Well?

MARIE.

Give me some money!   [*He gives her a gold piece.*] [MARIE *to her mother.*]   Here, here is money; now give me the linen ——

GYPSY.

[*Takes the money as she gives up the linen, greedily.*] A ducat!   A whole ducat!   A golden ducat!   Mine daughter, thank you!

MARIE.

And now, go!

GYPSY.

[*Goes anxiously to the door.*]   Alright, alright!!! [*Throws a kiss to* MARIE, *and quick exit.*]

MARIE.

[*Quickly takes key from board.*]   George, take this key and lock the garden gate after her, so she does not return.

[GEORGE *exits.* MARIE *looks after them, then slowly returns to the table, leans against same, and stares vacantly. Knock is heard at door L.*]

MARIE

[*Mechanically.*] Come in!

SERVANT.

[*Trying the door from the outside.*] The door is locked!

[MARIE *opens the door.*]

SERVANT.

[*Enters with dishes.*] It is time to lay the table for supper — will you help me, please? Why, what's the matter? You are not listening to me ——

MARIE.

Never mind, Lena, I will set the table myself!

SERVANT.

Will you? Very well!!! [*Exit* SERVANT.]

GEORGE.

[*Enters. To* MARIE, *who does not stir.*] Remember what I told you. But come, come, this will never do! Don't stare at me like that ——

MARIE.

[*Leaning on him and weeping.*] Oh, George!

GEORGE.

[*Stroking her hair.*] That's it, dear, the tears will relieve you! Ah, I well know the anguish of an aching heart!

MARIE.

Yes, you know, you know all! Now I have no one in this whole world but you — you alone. [*As she bursts out crying she throws herself on his breast.*]

THE FIRES OF ST. JOHN

GEORGE.

[*Stroking her hair.*]   Yes, yes; we two understand each other.   We two were meant, were intended for each other.   Were we not, dear?

MARIE.

My God!   Yes!!

GEORGE.

And we will ever remember this day — the day that brought us together.   It is the day before St. John's Eve.   Will you remember it, dear?

> [*Short pause.*   MARIE *silent, then struggles to free herself.*]

MARIE.

Don't, George!   Go away!   Please don't!

GEORGE.

[*Embarrassed.*]   But why should I suddenly go away, Marie?

MARIE.

Go, George, I beg of you!   I must lay the table!! Now go!

GEORGE.

Marie, you said yourself you had no one but me!

MARIE.

If you do not want to despise me, please go ——

GEORGE.

[*With forced laugh.*]   I despise you?   Very well — I'll go ——

> [*Turns once more in the door and hesitatingly exits.*]

> [MARIE *breaks down, weeping.*]
> [*Curtain.*]

END OF THE SECOND ACT.

ACT THREE

Same setting. Above the centre table a lighted hanging-lamp. Another lamp on table, L. The glass doors to garden are open. Full moonshine falls partly into the room. At rise of curtain, at table, L., are BRAUER, MRS. BRAUER *and* PASTOR. *At centre table,* GERTRUDE *and* GEORGE. *It is evening.*

BRAUER.

Now, then, tell Marie to bring the bowl!

PASTOR.

Ah! you are going to have a bowl?

MRS. BRAUER.

Why, of course, Pastor. This is St. John's Eve. The villagers will set off tar-barrels and bonfires, and we will celebrate it with a bowl.

BRAUER.

[*Mischievously.*] But perhaps this festival is too heathenish for the clergy ——

PASTOR.

Bless you, that all depends. If you have not the clergy's sanction, then it is wicked and heathenish ——

BRAUER.

But if they are invited, then it is Christianly and good? Ha, ha —— !

[75]

THE FIRES OF ST. JOHN

PASTOR.

Well, I did not say that. You had better apply to the consistory, they are better able to decide that point.

BRAUER.

Ah, Pastor, you are a diplomat. Well, what are you two doing over there? You are not saying a word.

GERTRUDE.

George is too lazy. He is drawing little men, and I am writing.

BRAUER.

In his place I think I would prefer to draw little women. Eh, Pastor?

GEORGE.

Just as you say, uncle!

BRAUER.

[*Aside.*] What the devil is the matter with him to-day? Come, children, be jolly, this is St. John's Eve! Ah, here is the punch! Now, then, Gertrude, lend a hand!

[MARIE *has entered with the bowl and glasses.*]

GERTRUDE.

Yes, papa.

BRAUER.

[*Drinks.*] Excellent, Marie! Superb! I tell you, Pastor, whoever gets her for a wife will be a lucky man indeed.

GERTRUDE.

[*With a glass to* GEORGE, *who has gone back and is looking out.*] Don't you want some, George?

GEORGE.

[*Caressing her, with a shy glance at* MARIE.] Why,

[76]

yes, little one, thank you! Look, how bright and beautiful the moon shines to-night! Everything wrapped as in silvery spider web! How beautiful!

MARIE.

[*Oppressed.*] They will soon set off the bonfires.

BRAUER.

See, see — at last you have spoken; I feared you had lost your tongue. Come here, my child. Get your glasses, all of you —— Your health! The Pastor shall give us a toast; yes, yes, Pastor! — a genuine pagan toast, well suited to this night! Now, tell me, my child, are you obliged to go to the city again to-night?

MARIE.

Yes, papa dear.

BRAUER.

But if I will not allow it?

MARIE.

You gave your permission quite two weeks ago, papa dear!

BRAUER

But not to go in the middle of the night!

MARIE.

I must go, papa. The men are to be there at seven in the morning, and if I am not there to give instructions the house will never be finished in time.

MRS. BRAUER.

Never mind, Henry, there is no help for it.

BRAUER.

But look at her!

MARIE.

Why, papa, there is nothing the matter with me. I am well and merry ——

BRAUER.

You are merry, eh? Let me hear you laugh!

MARIE.

[*Tries to laugh.*] Ha, ha, ha ——!

BRAUER.

[*Imitating her.*] Yes, yes — ha, ha, ha ——!

MRS. BRAUER.

Come here, my child. [*Strokes her hair.*] Did you
sleep well last night?

MARIE.

Yes, mama.

BRAUER.

But if this stranger should attack you again?

PASTOR.

Pardon me, but what do I hear?

BRAUER.

Oh, nothing of importance, Pastor. [*To* MARIE.]
You will take the one o'clock train ——

MARIE.

Yes, papa.

BRAUER.

There is another — at four — t'will be daylight
then ——

MARIE.

But I would not reach the city in time.

BRAUER.

Very well, you needn't go to bed, then. George can
take you to the depot.

MARIE.

[*Startled.*] George?

GEORGE.

[*Startled and simultaneously.*] What — I?

BRAUER.

Certainly! Why not?

PASTOR.

Pray do not think me obtrusive; but I am at your service.

BRAUER.

No, no, thank you, Pastor; your time will come some other day. [*Aside.*] It will at least give him something to do. [*Meaning* GEORGE.]

GERTRUDE.

I want to go too, papa! I love moonshine promenades.

BRAUER.

No, no, my pet. In the first place, it is very improper for lovers to be out so late at night, without a chaperon.

MARIE.

I would much prefer to go alone. I am not at all afraid — and I do not wish to trouble George — or any one else ——

BRAUER.

Any one else is out of the question, for in this house every one rises at five in the morning. [*To* GEORGE.] Now, then, what excuse have you to offer?

GEORGE.

Excuse? I? Why, none at all, except that she does not want me to go. You heard it yourself!

BRAUER.

Have you two been quarreling again?

MRS. BRAUER.

Don't insist, Henry, if they don't want to ——

BRAUER.

By the way, send for Mr. Paul — I wish to speak to him. Pastor, your health! [*Drinks.*]

[*At this* MARIE *and* GERTRUDE *go to door C., and speak to some one outside in pantomime. A voice is heard.*]

VOICE.

Mr. Paul! Mr. Paul!

PAUL.

[*From behind scene.*] I am coming in one moment! [*Short pause. He enters.*] Here I am!

BRAUER.

Ah, there you are! Give him a glass of punch!

PAUL.

Thank you, I have just had a glass of beer.

BRAUER.

Very well! Now, don't let us disturb you, children! Pastor, this is the time to prepare your toast. [*Aside to* PAUL.] Well, have you learned anything of this stranger?

PAUL.

Not a sign of one, excepting two tramps at the inn, the gendarme placed under arrest; but that was the day before yesterday.

BRAUER.

H'm! If I had ever had the slightest reason to doubt her word —— Marie, my child, come here to me.

MARIE.

Yes, papa!

BRAUER.

[*Looks at her sharply.*] Never mind, now.

PAUL.

[*Aside to* BRAUER.] By the way, I saw the old woman again!

BRAUER

Sh! not so loud! Where?

PAUL.

She had money, too ——

BRAUER.

I wonder where she stole it?

PAUL.

I wonder! The innkeeper said she had a gold piece. But don't you worry, Mr. Brauer. She will soon give us cause to have her locked up again. She is incorrigible!

BRAUER

Does she sleep at the inn?

PAUL.

No, sir! At night she leaves there, only to reappear in the morning.

BRAUER.

H'm! that would almost be sufficient reason —— George!

GEORGE.

Uncle?

BRAUER.

I have changed my mind. You must accompany Marie!

GEORGE.

Just as you say, uncle!

BRAUER.

And no quarreling this time, Marie!

MARIE.

Yes, papa.

THE FIRES OF ST. JOHN

GERTRUDE.

[*On the veranda.*] There, there, look! The first bonfire!!

[*Singing and laughter is heard in distance. A red glow is seen.*]

MRS. BRAUER.

Have you taken care, Mr. Paul, to keep them far enough away from the sheds?

PAUL.

Yes, Mrs. Brauer!

MRS. BRAUER.

For you must know, Pastor, last year the sparks came very near setting fire to the straw roofs.

GERTRUDE.

There is a second one now, and there on the hill, another. See, George, see! How beautiful!

GEORGE.

Yes, yes, darling, I see!

GERTRUDE.

[*Pulls him forward softly.*] Why do you call me darling to-day?

GEORGE.

Well, shan't I?

GERTRUDE.

Oh, of course; but do you love me more to-day?

GEORGE.

I love you always, my pet!

GERTRUDE.

[*Softly and with emotion.*] But you usually call me "little one," and to-day nothing but "darling."

BRAUER.

Now, then, Pastor, we are ready for the toast! Take up your glass, and fire away!

[82]

PASTOR.

I am afraid it will be hardly as wicked and heathenish as you seem to expect.

BRAUER.

Come, come, Pastor, don't keep us waiting!

PASTOR.

Well, what shall I say? I am not going to preach you a sermon!

BRAUER.

No, no, Pastor; we are content to wait for that till Sunday.

PASTOR.

Well, then, you see, on a beautiful and dreamy night like this — may I say dreamy?

BRAUER.

You may, Pastor, you may!

PASTOR.

For we all dream at times, more or less, both young and old —— !

BRAUER.

Ah, yes! that is a failing we all have!!!

PASTOR.

On such a dreamy night, different emotions are aroused within us. We seem to be able to look into the future, and imagine ourselves able to fathom all mystery and heal all wounds. The common becomes elevated, our wishes become fate; and now we ask ourselves: What is it that causes all this within us — all these desires and wishes? It is *love*, brotherly love, that has been planted in our souls, that fills our lives; and, it is life itself. Am I not right? And now, with one bound, I will come to the point. In the revelation you will find: "God is love." Yes, God is love; and that is the most beautiful trait of our religion — that the best, the most beautiful within us, has been granted us by *Him* above. Then how could I, this very evening, so overcome with feeling for my fellow-man — how could I pass *Him* by? Therefore, Mr. Brauer, no matter, whether pastor or layman, I must confess my inability to grant your wish, and decline to give you a genuine pagan toast——

BRAUER.

[*Grasps his hand.*] That was well spoken, Pastor! Pardon me, I was only jesting!

GEORGE.

No, no, dear uncle, not altogether. There I must defend you against yourself. A devout and pious man like yourself, t'was not entire wantonness, your desire to hear something other than religious, and since the Pastor has so eloquently withdrawn, I will give you a toast. For, you see, my dear Pastor, something of the old pagan, a spark of heathenism, is still glowing somewhere within us all. It has outlived century after century, from the time of the old Teutons. Once every year that spark is fanned into flame — it flames up high, and then it is called "The Fires of St. John." Once every year we have "free night." Then the witches ride upon their brooms — the same brooms with which their witchcraft was once driven out of them — with scornful laughter the wild hordes sweep across the tree-tops, up, up, high upon the Blocksberg! Then it is, when in our hearts awake those wild desires which our fates could not fulfill — and, understand me well, dared not fulfill — then, no matter what may be the name of the law that governs the world on that day, in order that that one single wish may become a reality, by whose grace we prolong our miserable existence, thousand others must miserably perish. Part because they were never attainable; but the others, yes, the others, because we allowed them to escape us like wild birds, which, though already in our hands, but too listless to profit by opportunity, we failed to grasp at the right moment. But no matter. Once every year we have "free night." And yonder tongues of fire shooting up towards the heavens — do you know what they are? They are the spirits of our dead and perished wishes! That is the red plumage of our birds of paradise we might have petted and nursed through our entire lives, but have escaped us! That is the old chaos, the heathenism within us; and though we be happy in sunshine and according to law, to-night is St. John's night. To its ancient pagan fires I empty this glass. To-night they shall burn and flame up high — high — and again high ——! Will no one drink to my toast?

[*Pause.*]

MARIE.

[*Trembling.*] I will!

> [*They look into each other's eyes and clink glasses.*]

GERTRUDE.

[*Hesitatingly.*] I, too, George!

GEORGE.

[*Stroking her hair sadly, patronizing.*] Yes, yes; you, too.

BRAUER.

[*Suddenly bursting out.*] You — you idiots! What do you know about it, anyway? I — I didn't understand it myself, but I have a presentiment there is something sinful about it all!

[85]

THE FIRES OF ST. JOHN

PASTOR.

My dear Mr. von Harten, above all your heathenism watches our good old God, our Father, and therefore I fearlessly drink to your toast.

BRAUER.

Well, well, I'll not be the only exception. [*Drinks also. A glow much nearer, behind the trees. Louder yelling and laughter.*] Well, what is it now?

PAUL.

They are dangerously near the sheds now.

BRAUER.

Didn't I tell you to take the proper precautions?

PAUL.

I did. They had only three tar-barrels early this evening. Where they got the fourth from, I don't know.

BRAUER.

I'll wager they found the barrel of axle-grease! Why didn't you lock it up?

PAUL.

You know yourself, on this day no lock or key is of any avail.

BRAUER.

Don't talk nonsense, but see what's to be done. I will be there myself, presently. Be quick! [PAUL *exits*.] I can't depend on anybody these days! Where is my hat? [MARIE *gets it*.]

GERTRUDE.

Can't we go, too, papa?

BRAUER.

Will you come, wife?

[86]

MRS. BRAUER.

Yes, gladly, but stop scolding. There isn't a breath of air stirring, and therefore no danger.

BRAUER.

Come along, Pastor!

[*Exit* BRAUER, GEORGE, GERTRUDE and MRS. BRAUER.]

PASTOR.

Won't you accompany us, Miss Marie?

MARIE.

No, thank you, Pastor!

PASTOR.

Then may I remain with you for a while?

SEVERAL VOICES.

[*Outside, calling.*] Pastor, Pastor!

PASTOR.

[*Speaks through door.*] I will be with you in a moment! [*To* MARIE.] Well, may I!

MARIE.

Why, certainly, if it gives you pleasure!

PASTOR.

Pleasure is hardly the proper word. I wanted to thank you for insisting upon my writing the bridal-poem. It has been a work of pleasure, I assure you. Do you like it?

MARIE.

It is very nice, Pastor!

PASTOR.

Have you memorized it already?

MARIE.

I think so!

THE FIRES OF ST. JOHN

PASTOR.

Then would you mind reciting it for me? Come, I will assist you: "The flowers, the beautiful blossoms" —— Well? —— "are a maiden's ——"

MARIE.

No, Pastor!

PASTOR.

You are acting so strangely to-day! You are so shy — so ——.

MARIE.

The St. John's night oppresses me!

PASTOR.

That will soon be over.

MARIE.

Would that it were over now!

PASTOR.

Perhaps the thought of traveling alone at night has something to do with it?

MARIE.

Oh! [*Recovering herself — lightly.*] You are right, Pastor; but it can't be helped!

PASTOR.

Shall I come with you? Oh, I'll find something to be done in the city. I won't even have to ask permission. Anyway, I am longing for a glimpse of the good old town. I will inform the old pastor — I don't think he has retired as yet ——

MARIE.

Then please tell him —— I usually visit him myself every day, but now, just before the wedding, it's impossible for me to call. Will you please tell him that? I am so fond of him! Tell him that, and in thought I kiss his hand.

PASTOR.

Certainly. And may I accompany you!

MARIE.

No, thank you, Pastor!

PASTOR.

Now let us speak openly, Miss Marie. I have been watching you all the evening. You appear to me — what shall I call it — like a mouse before a cat! You need a protector; some one in whom you can confide, some one ——

MARIE.

And so you would like to be my father confessor! Eh, Pastor?

PASTOR.

You know very well we do not have that institution in the Protestant Church, though at times it might prove a blessing ——

MARIE.

[*Mischievously.*] And then again it might not?

PASTOR.

You are quite right. We should all rely more upon ourselves ——

MARIE.

[*With emphasis.*] I do that, Pastor, I do!

PASTOR.

Yes, my dear Marie pardon me, I should not have said that — and yet I must speak frankly with you; you seem to have a fear — a dread ——

MARIE.

Of the cat ?

PASTOR.

I wish I knew ! ! !

MARIE.

But supposing I were the cat, who would then be the mouse?

PASTOR.

That would be sinful and wicked in you ! ! !

MARIE.

But one cannot be the cat and the mouse at the same time?

PASTOR.

Yes, one can! But he who does, plays with his own destruction!

MARIE.

And if one destroys one's self, who cares?

PASTOR.

You should not talk like that, Miss Marie.

MARIE.

Oh, it is all nonsense, all nonsense, for to-night is St. John's night. Do you see that fire yonder, Pastor? They had to put it out! But there, on the hill — look, there, there! How beautiful! How wild!

PASTOR.

Yes, and when you look closely, it is nothing more than a mass of dirty lumber.

MARIE.

For shame, Pastor!

PASTOR.

Like everything that blazes, except the sun ——

MARIE.

You should not have said that, Pastor — you should not. I don't want it! I will not have you slander my

St. John's fires! I want to enjoy it once — only once —
then nevermore ! ! !

PASTOR.

[*Disturbed.*] My dear Miss Marie, I do not understand the reason for your agitation, and I will not
question you! But of your struggles — you shall know
that you have a friend near you, on whom you can rely,
now and for all time to come. Marie, I don't know how
to express myself; but I desire to shield and protect
you all your life — I will worship you ——

MARIE.

Pastor, do you know who and what I am?

PASTOR.

I do!

MARIE.

And who my mother is?

PASTOR.

I know all!

MARIE.

Pastor, how am I to understand this?

PASTOR.

Marie, I know I should not have spoken, at least not
now. I should have waited — it was stupid of me, I
know; but I have such a fear — a fear for you. You
are going to the city to-night and I don't know what
may happen! But you shall know before you go, where
you belong and that your future is assured!

MARIE.

[*With a sigh of relief — almost a sob.*] Ah — ah —
ah —— !

PASTOR.

Marie, I do not want an answer now. Besides, I must

first notify my father. Though he is but a simple farmer, he shall not be slighted —— Marie ——

MARIE.

[*Shrinking — dully.*]   Yes, that is — perhaps —what I need — ah! [*Sinks in chair.*]

PASTOR.

Why, what is the matter? Shall I get you a glass of water? Or would you prefer wine?

MARIE.

[*With an effort.*]   Wine — wine — there — in the bowl! [*He helps her — she drinks.*]   Thank you! [*Stirred.*]   No one has ever waited on me before!

PASTOR.

I will carry you upon my hands ——

MARIE.

Very well, Pastor; but no one must know before the wedding!

PASTOR.

Perhaps on the wedding day — at the wedding feast? Papa might make the announcement; that would be such a fitting occasion!

MARIE.

No, no! I will have to much to do then.

PASTOR.

Then, when the happy pair have gone?

MARIE.

[*With sudden, impulsive decision.*]   Yes, when they have gone!

PASTOR.

[*Takes her hand.*]   Thank you, Miss Marie.

[*Voices are heard outside.*]

MARIE.

Sh — [*Withdrawing her hand.*]

GERTRUDE.

[*Enters.*]   Ah, here you are, Pastor; we have been looking for you everywhere!

PASTOR.

I am coming now, Miss Gertrude.

GERTRUDE.

It's too late, Pastor, they are all returning!

PASTOR.

Impossible!   Well, well, how the time passes, and one hardly knows how!

[*Exit* PASTOR.]

MARIE.

[*Embracing* GERTRUDE.]   Will you forgive me, darling?

GERTRUDE.

[*Timidly.*]   I have nothing to forgive!

MARIE.

Do not say that!   I have done everything — everything — you must ——

[*Enter all.*]

BRAUER.

Well, my dear Pastor, time stands still for no one; so you had better stop excusing yourself and empty your glass.   'Twill all come out right in the end.

PASTOR.

I think I had better go now; for here every one is making fun of me.

BRAUER.

Pastor, I need hardly tell you, that you are always welcome in this house.

THE FIRES OF ST. JOHN

PASTOR.

I am sure of it, Mr. Brauer! If I did not think so, I would not take that matter so lightly ——

BRAUER.

[*Jokingly threatens him with finger.*] Pastor ——

PASTOR.

[*With a happy glance at* MARIE.] Good-night. [*Shakes hands with all.*]

BRAUER.

Good-night!

PASTOR.

Good-night, Miss Marie!

MARIE.

[*Shaking his hand.*] Good-night, Pastor!

[GEORGE, *with a questioning glance, advances a step or two.*]

BRAUER.

George, see the Pastor to the gate!

GEORGE.

[*As though awakening.*] Yes, uncle.

[*Both exit.*]

MRS. BRAUER.

Well, Henry, everything has quieted down!

BRAUER.

It's about time, too! Why, its eleven o'clock! Come, let's to bed.

GERTRUDE.

Good-night, papa!

BRAUER.

[*Affectionately.*] Good-night, my pet!

MARIE.

Good-night!

BRAUER.

By the bye — when will you be back?

MARIE.

To-morrow, about ten, papa!

BRAUER.

Now be careful; no unnecessary exertions — understand? The day of the wedding will be hard enough on all of us.

MARIE.

Yes, papa dear! [*Kisses him.*]

GEORGE.

[*Enters at this moment.*] We have still an hour and a quarter till train time. I will wait for you here, Marie.

MRS. BRAUER

You might help each other pass away the time.

GERTRUDE.

I want to sit up, too.

BRAUER.

Tut, tut, my pet; you go to bed, you need the rest.

GERTRUDE.

[*Whiningly.*] Well then, good-night.

MARIE.

[*In silent fear.*] I can't stay here —— Mama, I want to ask you about something ——

GEORGE.

Then you will come down in time for the train?

MARIE.

Yes, in time for the train.

MRS. BRAUER.

Good-night, George.

THE FIRES OF ST. JOHN

GEORGE.

Good-night, auntie!

[*Exit* MRS. BRAUER, GERTRUDE *and* MARIE.]

BRAUER.

You know where my cigars are?

GEORGE.

Yes!

BRAUER.

And if you need anything to keep you awake — I have left the key ——

GEORGE.

[*In monosyllables.*] Thank you!

BRAUER.

Well, what in — —

GEORGE.

What's the matter —— Oh, my dear uncle, if I have failed to pay you the necessary respect, I beg your pardon.

BRAUER.

Respect? Oh, damn you and your respect!

GEORGE.

Uncle ——

BRAUER.

See here, perhaps I did wrong?

GEORGE.

You — wrong? How?

BRAUER.

Have you forgotten what passed between us yesterday?

GEORGE.

My dear uncle, that seems to me so far, far away!

THE FIRES OF ST. JOHN

BRAUER.

It strikes me you are going at a pretty fast gait!

GEORGE.

At any rate, uncle, do not worry about it. It will all come out right in the end. [*As he is listening towards the door, gives a sudden start.*]

BRAUER.

What's the matter?

GEORGE.

I thought I heard some one ——

BRAUER.

Some one of the family perhaps, upstairs. Very well, then all is well, my boy! Good-night, my son.

GEORGE.

Good-night, uncle!

[BRAUER *exits, shaking his head.*]

GEORGE.

[*Sits at table — tries to read — listens, goes to door C.—calls out softly into the garden.*] Who is there? [*Still softer.*] Is that you, Marie?

GERTRUDE.

[*Whining outside.*] It's only me!

GEORGE.

[*Surprised.*] Gertrude, what do you want?

GERTRUDE.

[GERTRUDE *enters in nightgown and flowing hair.*] I am so uneasy, George dear; I just wanted to look at you once more before going to sleep.

GEORGE.

But, little one, if papa should see you like this —— Quick, go back to your room.

[97]

THE FIRES OF ST. JOHN

GERTRUDE.

I cannot, my heart is so heavy.

GEORGE

How so, dear?

GERTRUDE.

George, I have been thinking; I really am not good enough to be your wife.

GEORGE.

Wha — what nonsense ——

GERTRUDE.

I am too silly — oh, yes; I never know what to say to you! I am so stupid.

GEORGE.

Why, my child — darling — pet ——

GERTRUDE.

A while ago, out in the garden, and the moon shining so brightly, you walked by my side in deep silence ——

GEORGE.

Why, mama was with us ——

GERTRUDE.

George, it is yet time. If you love some one else ——

GEORGE.

In heaven's name, child, have you ever mentioned this to any one?

GERTRUDE.

Only to papa; he was very angry and scolded me dreadfully.

GEORGE.

H'm! Now listen to me, my pet ——

[98]

GERTRUDE.

Rather than make you unhappy, I would jump into the river ——

GEORGE.

In the first place, your presence here in this condition is decidedly improper ——

GERTRUDE.

But we are to be married in three days ——

GEORGE.

So much more reason. [*Stroking her hair.*] What beautiful hair you have, dear!

GERTRUDE.

[*Happily.*] Do you like it?

GEORGE.

And in the second place, I will have none other than you. We will love each other very much. At first you will be my playmate — and then — later, perhaps — my real mate. Are you satisfied?

GERTRUDE.

Yes, dear!

GEORGE.

And now, you must go to bed!

GERTRUDE.

Then I will wrap myself in my hair — and I will dream of you and what you said — that it is beautiful — and so I will fall asleep. Good-night, George dear!

GEORGE.

[*Kisses her on the forehead.*] Good-night!
[*He gloomily takes position at table with a sigh when* GERTRUDE *exits, covering his face with his hands.* MARIE *enters softly.*]

THE FIRES OF ST. JOHN

GEORGE.

Marie, you have come ——

MARIE.

It is early yet, is it not?

GEORGE.

We have a full hour more. Have they all gone to bed?

MARIE.

I think so. All the lights are out.

GEORGE.

Come, sit here ——

MARIE.

I — I — I think I will go back upstairs!

GEORGE.

No, no; here is something to read! You see, I'm reading myself.

MARIE.

Very well. [*Sits.*] But, George, I would really prefer to go to the depot alone.

GEORGE.

[*Softly.*] Marie! [*She shuts her eyes.*] Are you tired? [*She shakes her head.*] One whole hour I will have you all to myself!

MARIE.

George ——

GEORGE.

Marie ! ! !

MARIE.

The fires have all gone out, I suppose?

GEORGE.

Ah, yes; a small pyre of wood — it is soon burned down!

MARIE.

And then it's as dark as ever!!! But, George, how beautifully you spoke this evening! I have never heard anything like it before.

GEORGE.

You were the only one who understood me.

MARIE.

No wonder! It was as though I spoke the words myself — that is, I don't mean to say ——

GEORGE.

What, dear?

MARIE.

Oh, you know!

GEORGE.

But I don't know!

MARIE.

[*After a pause.*] George, I have something to confess to you. In fact, that is why I came down here so soon. You shall know it, you alone. I have this day given my hand ——

GEORGE.

[*With a start.*] *Marie!!!!*

MARIE.

[*Astonished.*] Well?

GEORGE.

To whom?

MARIE.

Why, to the pastor! Who else could it be? There is no one else!

GEORGE.

[*Reproachfully.*] Why did you do that? Why did you?

THE FIRES OF ST. JOHN

MARIE.

I have my whole life before me, and the fires [*pointing to fields and to heart*] will not burn forever ——

GEORGE.

[*Bitterly.*] You should not have done it — you — it is a ——

MARIE.

Sh — not so loud!

GEORGE.

But you do not love him at all!!!!

MARIE.

How do you know?

GEORGE.

[*Bitterly.*] How? Of course, how should I? I don't know! Pardon me! Well, I congratulate you!

MARIE.

[*Quietly.*] Thank you!

GEORGE.

But why am I the first one to be taken into your confidence? Why not uncle? We two have not been so intimate as ——

MARIE.

No, we two have not been very intimate — I only thought ——

GEORGE.

So, then, we have both our burden; and we soon will have to part. Therefore we can now safely speak of the past. My manuscript you read! You even went so far as to perjure yourself on account of it. Oh, you don't mind a little thing like that! I wish I were the same! You know the subject of my verses, and we must now understand each other fully. Now, tell me openly, why, why did you treat me so unkindly, to say nothing worse, in former days?

MARIE.

Did I, George?

GEORGE.

'Tis hardly necessary to remind you of all the indignities you heaped upon me. It almost seemed to me as if you purposely intended to drive me mad. Do you remember the day when I followed you into the cellar, and you turned and ran out and locked the door, and compelled me to remain there all night?

MARIE.

[*Smiling.*] Yes, I remember!

GEORGE.

Why did you do that?

MARIE.

That is very simple. You are Count von Harten — and I? — I am but a poor Lithuanian foundling — aye, worse than that. If you follow such a one into the cellar, she knows, or at least thinks she knows, your purpose.

GEORGE.

So, that was the reason! And at the same time you went under your manzanillo-tree to die?

MARIE.

[*Nods.*]

GEORGE.

And did you never realize the real state of things? Gertrude was then still a child — and because I could not win you, I took her. Did that thought never occur to you?

[103]

MARIE.

How could I ever dare to think that?

GEORGE.

But later?

MARIE.

The day before yesterday, when I read your book, I felt it for the first time.

GEORGE.

And now, it is too late ——

MARIE.

Yes, now it is too late! Had I felt then as I do now, I would not have resisted you ——

GEORGE.

Marie, do you know what you are saying?

MARIE.

[*Breaking out.*] Oh I don't care, I don't care! It is my fate. You must rule and govern — and I — I must serve; and in the end — we both must die ——

GEORGE.

Marie, you should be loved, you must be loved — beyond all senses — loved beyond all measure!

MARIE.

[*Pointing towards R.*] He loves me!

GEORGE.

He? — Bah!!!

MARIE.

Don't be angry, George dear; you don't dare love me yourself. You can never be anything to me!

GEORGE.

No, never; for this house must be kept clean. No, no, this house must not be soiled. We would both suffocate in our shame. But we can think of what might have been; that is not sin, is it?

MARIE.

What were your words? "They are the wild birds of paradise, that have escaped us." That was it, was it not? How beautiful!

GEORGE.

I don't remember!

MARIE.

But I am not a wild bird, George; I am tame — so tame ——

GEORGE.

You are tame?

MARIE.

For you, George dear, only for you!!!

GEORGE.

Marie, my love! [*Strokes her hair affectionally, then moves away.*] No, no, we must be strong! Only a few minutes ago, Gertrude came softly down those stairs; if she should come again — my God——!

MARIE.

What did she want?

GEORGE.

You can imagine ——

MARIE.

The poor thing! But you will love her?

GEORGE.

As well as possible! But then I must not think of you.

MARIE.

But you must not think of me — and I will try and not think of you!

THE FIRES OF ST. JOHN

GEORGE.

Never, Marie?

MARIE.

Only occasionally — on holidays ——

GEORGE.

Only then?

MARIE.

And on St. John's eve ——

GEORGE.

When the fires are burning?

MARIE.

Yes, and when the fires are out, then I shall cry ——

GEORGE.

Marie ! ! ! !

MARIE.

No, no, George, sit still — I will sit here. Some one might be in the garden, after all.

GEORGE.

They are all sound asleep !

MARIE.

Even so ! We must be brave; not for mine — but for your sake, George.

GEORGE.

Why did you say that? What do you think of me?

MARIE.

I think you are hard-hearted.

GEORGE.

And yet you love me?

MARIE.

Yes, I love you, for your own sake. For you have had to struggle and fight — and that is what made you what you are. I have also fought and struggled; but I have lost faith in myself — lost faith in everything. If you only knew!! Sometimes I am afraid of myself — sometimes I would commit murder, so restless and without peace I am.

GEORGE.

With me you would have found peace. We would have worked together and planned through half the nights — and you know how ambitious I am.

MARIE.

And so am I, for you! You should be the first and greatest. They all shall bow before you — I myself will kneel before you and say to you: "You love to rule and command? Now rule — now command!!!!!!"

[*Throws herself before him — her arms around his knees, looking up.*]

GEORGE.

Marie, in heaven's name rise! If any one should see you so ——

MARIE.

Let them see me ——

GEORGE.

Marie!!

MARIE.

[*Rising.*] You are right. It was low in me. But he who originates where I do, is low — so low ——

GEORGE.

Don't think of it, Marie! Think of this house and all the love it has given you!

MARIE.

How quiet everything is — not a sound to be heard — as silent as the grave ——

GEORGE.

Then be content, for they have buried us together!

MARIE.

If they only had ——!

GEORGE.

And see the pale moon — how it throws its silvery rays over the garden — and yonder is your manzanillo-tree.

MARIE.

Yes, yes, do you see it?

GEORGE.

And its white, trembling leaves; see, see, each one seems alive — though not a breath of air is stirring. Come, let us go to it.

MARIE.

[*Cowering.*] No, no, I think it is time — we must ——

GEORGE.

Sh! — Sh ——!

MARIE.

What is it?

GEORGE.

There — something moved. It must be Gertrude. [*Goes to door C. and calls.*] "Gertrude!!!"

[*Short pause.*]

MARIE.

You must have been mistaken!

GEORGE.

No, no; I saw a shadow. "Gertrude!" Remain here, I'll go see! [*Exit into garden.*]

MARIE.

Oh, I'm so afraid, George — so afraid ——!

[*Pause.*]

[GEORGE *returns, pale and agitated, trying to control himself.*]

MARIE.

Who was it? Who was it?

GEORGE.

Oh, no one — no one ——

MARIE.

Yes, there was — I can see it in your face!! Was it Gertrude?

GEORGE.

No.

MARIE.

Then it was papa?

GEORGE.

No, no.

MARIE.

George, you are as pale as death; What has happened? Tell me!

GEORGE.

Nothing, nothing! There was a stranger in the garden — I sent him away.

MARIE.

What stranger?

GEORGE.

[*Pained.*] Do not ask me!

MARIE.

[*Dully.*] Oh, I know — I know! It was — my mother ——

GEORGE.

Well, since you have said it ——

MARIE.

What did she want? But why do I ask? [*Covers her face with her hands.*] Oh, my God — my God!!!!

GEORGE.

Marie!

THE FIRES OF ST. JOHN

MARIE.

[*Suddenly*.]   Close the blinds — I have a fear — tight — so ! !   Now put up the bars — so — and here, so — so ——

GEORGE.

[*Embracing her*.]   *Marie !* my darling ! ! ! !

MARIE.

Hold me tight ! ! !

GEORGE.

Like this ?

MARIE.

Yes, like that !   [*She moves close to him*.]   Here I want to sit still ——

GEORGE.

[*Looks at watch*.]   If we only have time to catch that train ——   [*The whistle of a locomotive is heard in the distance.   He starts*.]   Did you hear that ?

MARIE.

[*Smilingly*.]   Yes !

GEORGE.

What was it ?

MARIE.

It was the train !

GEORGE.

Can you hear it this far ?

MARIE.

At night you can !

GEORGE.

[*Sinks into chair L. of table, back to audience*.]
My God ! what shall we do now ?

MARIE.

[*Softly*.] I will tell you what we will do! We will sit still here — quietly — till the next train — till four o'clock!!!!

> [*Throws herself upon George, passionately kissing him.*]

GEORGE.

Marie! My love, my all! [*Kisses her.*]

MARIE.

Kiss me again! Now, then, do you understand me? I am my own master, and care not for myself —— To-night is St. John's night!!!!!!!

GEORGE.

And the fires are burning low ——

MARIE.

No, no; let them burn ——

GEORGE.

Yes, yes; let them burn — they shall burn!!!!!

> [*Marie disengages herself.*]

MARIE.

Kiss me no more — let me kiss you — I will take all upon myself — I will take all the consequences — *my mother is a thief, and so am I! George* ——

> [*Throws herself into his arms with complete abandon.*]

> [*Lights out. Curtain.*]

END OF THE THIRD ACT.

ACT FOUR

Same setting. Morning. Centre table is decorated with flowers. BRAUER, GEORGE *and* GERTRUDE *are on veranda at rise of curtain. In open door, C.,* MRS. BRAUER. *All listening to quartet, singing, " This is the day of our Lord," by Kreutzer. As curtain rises,* KATIE *enters, L., listens also, and dries her eyes. At the end of the serenade,* BRAUER *starts to make an address, and with* GEORGE *and* GERTRUDE *leaves the veranda.*

KATIE.

Mrs. Brauer, I would like to speak to you a moment.

MRS. BRAUER.

[*Wiping her eyes.*]   What is it, Katie?

KATIE.

[*Sniveling.*]   Oh, I'm so happy ——
    [*Church bells are heard softly in the distance.*]

MRS. BRAUER.

There go the church bells.   Have you put plenty of wine and luncheon in the arbor?

KATIE.

Yes, ma'am!   Miss Marie and I have prepared a lot!

MRS. BRAUER.

What did you want to see me about?

THE FIRES OF ST. JOHN

KATIE.

I wanted to ask you about the roast; shall we put it in the oven now, and just warm it up for dinner? Miss Marie thinks——

MRS. BRAUER.

Never mind! I'll be down in the kitchen in a moment!

KATIE.

And another thing, Mrs. Brauer; won't you please try and get Miss Marie to take a little rest? She has been hard at work since two o'clock this morning, and all day yesterday she was in the city. She can't stand it.

MRS. BRAUER.

Oh, on a day like this, we must all put our shoulders to the wheel.

KATIE.

Ah, Mrs. Brauer, you and I are old, and not much good for anything but work; but we must spare our young people. Why, at times she almost gives out.

MRS. BRAUER.

Well, I will come and see for myself.

KATIE.

Thank you!!! Oh, such a day!!! I am so happy —— [*Exit both L.*]

BRAUER.

[*Enters with* GEORGE *and* GERTRUDE.] Thank goodness, that's over. Let me see: first it was the old soldiers, then the Turners, and now the Singing Society —— But do you know, I am so sick of all this wine — give me a brandy.

GERTRUDE.

[*Gets drink from sideboard.*] Yes, papa!

[113]

THE FIRES OF ST. JOHN

BRAUER.

[*To* GEORGE.]   And what's the matter with you?

GEORGE

[*With a sigh.*]   Nothing!

BRAUER.

[*Imitating him.*]   Nothing!!!   I can't quite make you out —— Here, have a drink?

GEORGE.

No, thank you!

BRAUER.

Well, then, don't!   Your health, my pet!

GERTRUDE.

Drink hearty, papa!

BRAUER.

[*Rises.*]   The carriage will arrive here sharply at ten!   Understand?

GEORGE.

Yes!

BRAUER.

And your friend from the city — we will find him at the station?

GEORGE.

Yes; he arrives quarter to ten.

BRAUER.

For we must have two witnesses. — Do you know what I would like?   [*Tapping him on breast.*]   I would like to be able to look in there.

GERTRUDE.

Oh, let him alone, papa!   He is now my George.   If I am satisfied with him ——

[114]

BRAUER.

You are right! He who gets my child can laugh — but he also *shall* laugh. Understand? [*Exit R.*]

GERTRUDE.

Never mind him, George dear. You need not laugh if you don't want to. Not on my account. [*Bells.*] Do you hear, George? The church bells, ringing softly, singing, like human voices!!!! That is for you and me!!

GEORGE.

Why for us?

GERTRUDE.

It is the old pastor's desire; half an hour this morning, and then again this afternoon, when we exchange rings. Do you know, George, mama says a bride's dream the night before her wedding is surely an omen. Do you believe that?

GEORGE.

[*Preoccupied.*] Yes.

GERTRUDE.

I dreamed last night of a large, yellow wheat-field, in which a poor little rabbit had hidden itself; and high above, in the air, I saw a large hawk. Then it appeared to me that I was the little rabbit, and in fear and dread I called out "George! George!" when suddenly it shot down upon me! — just think ——

GEORGE.

And then?

GERTRUDE.

Then I awoke. The cold perspiration stood thickly upon my brow —— Oh, George dear, you will protect me? You won't let any one hurt me, will you? For I am only a poor little rabbit, after all ——

GEORGE.

[*Staring before him.*] My God!

GERTRUDE.

George, I wanted to ask you something.

GEORGE.

Well?

GERTRUDE.

You don't love some one else, do you?

GEORGE.

[*Disturbed.*] But, my child ——

GERTRUDE.

Well, you know that if a bride cannot laugh on her wedding day, she loves another ——

GEORGE.

Why, nonsense ——

GERTRUDE.

[*Unshaken.*] Oh, yes, George; I read it myself. And even if you do, George, I feel so — my love for you is so great, it could move mountains. I love you so dearly —— She will surely learn to forget you, I will love you so much.

GEORGE.

But, my pet ——

GERTRUDE.

No, no, George. You see, I don't blame you so much. How could I? For what am I, compared to other women? — George, does she love you so very much?

GEORGE.

Who?

GERTRUDE.

Oh, you know. But don't worry, George dear; she will forget you in time! Don't you remember Robert, our neighbor's son? He threatened to kill himself if I didn't marry him, and he has already forgotten me! And to-day, when we stand at the altar, at the Doxology and the exchange of rings, I will nudge you softly, and then we will both pray to our good Father in heaven to make it easy for her; for no one shall be unhappy on this day! Why, George, you are crying!!!!

GEORGE.

Crying — I?

GERTRUDE.

Why, yes! Here are two large tears runnning down your cheek. [*Wipes his eyes with her handkerchief.*] So there ——

GEORGE.

Tell me, my pet, and if we should be parted, after all?

GERTRUDE.

How could that be possible?

GEORGE.

If I should die — or ——

GERTRUDE.

[*Embracing him.*] No, no! Don't say that! Don't say that!!!

[MARIE *appears in door, seeing embrace.*]

GEORGE.

[*Startled.*] Some one is here ——

GERTRUDE.

It is only Marie.

MARIE.

[*Pointedly.*] You seem to be particularly affectionate to-day.

THE FIRES OF ST. JOHN

GERTRUDE.

[*Miffed.*] We always love each other. Oh, perhaps that doesn't please you ——

MARIE.

It is nothing to me !

GERTRUDE.

[*Half jesting.*] Besides, what do you want here? Isn't there anything to do in the kitchen?

MARIE.

[*Stung, but controlling herself.*] Mama has sent me ——

GERTRUDE.

Yes, yes, dear; you are just in time to dress my hair. Have you hairpins?

MARIE.

[*Shaking her head.*] I will get some. [*Reels.*]

GERTRUDE.

[*Affectionately.*] What's the matter, dear? Oh, you must be tired !

MARIE.

I am not tired.

GERTRUDE.

Yes, yes, you are. Now you sit down here. I will fetch them myself.   [*Quick exit.*]

MARIE.

[*Full of fear.*] Gertrude ! ! !

GEORGE.

I must speak with you !

MARIE.

Speak; I am listening.

GEORGE.

Why this tone? Does it perhaps mean that between us all is over?

MARIE.

If it is or is not, it matters little.

GEORGE.

Am I, then, to understand ——

MARIE.

My God! Have you not Gertrude? But now I saw her in your arms! What do you want with me?

GEORGE.

I must speak with you ——

MARIE.

Not now ——

GERTRUDE.

[*Re-enters.*] Here are the hairpins. [MARIE *takes them.*] I have also brought my dressing-sacque and combs. Now we will excuse you for a little while, George dear. You can give your judgment later.

GEORGE.

[*With a glance at* MARIE.] May I not remain?

GERTRUDE.

No, no. You would criticise and find fault, and embarrass Marie, and me, too. Now be good, George, and go into the garden. [GEORGE *exits.*]

MARIE.

[*Holding sacque.*] Will you put this on?

GERTRUDE.

No, I will put it around me.

MARIE.

As you please. How do you want your hair dressed, high or low?

GERTRUDE.

But Marie, we had decided upon that! Have you forgotten?

[119]

THE FIRES OF ST. JOHN

MARIE.

Oh, pardon me — I — of course we had!

GERTRUDE.

Then give me a kiss!

> [MARIE *suddenly takes her head in both hands and stares at her.*]

GERTRUDE.

[*Frightened.*]   Why do you look at me so strangely?

MARIE.

[*Embraces her fiercely.*]   My darling!!!!

GERTRUDE.

Oh, you hurt me!

MARIE.

Perhaps you hurt me, too ——

GERTRUDE.

I?   How so?

MARIE.

[*Has begun to comb.*]   How can you ask?   You are about to be married — and — and — I — I am jealous of you!

GERTRUDE.

Just wait, Marie, dear.   [*Sings.*]
" In a year, in a year, when the nightingale comes ——"

MARIE.

[*Intensely.*]   When the nightingale comes?

GERTRUDE.

You will be Pastor's wife.   [*Laughs.*]

> [MARIE, *with one braid in her hand, bending back, laughing loudly and forced.*]

GERTRUDE.

[*In pain.*]   Oh, you are pulling my hair ——

THE FIRES OF ST. JOHN

MARIE.

Any one as happy as you should be able to bear a
a little pain. There! I will braid it into your hair —
for you are happy, are you not? Very happy?

GERTRUDE.

Yes! I am — that is — I would like to be — but
George — he is so sad.

MARIE.

George?

GERTRUDE.

Yes!

MARIE.

[*Lurkingly.*] Perhaps you were right! Perhaps he
does love another!

GERTRUDE.

[*Softly groaning.*] Oh, why did you say that?

MARIE.

Because —— No, no — how could he? That was
wicked in me, wasn't it? How could he think of
another, when he looks at you?

GERTRUDE.

No, no, Marie, you are right! I told him so myself!

MARIE.

[*Slowly and marked.*] And what did he say?

GERTRUDE.

He? — He said nothing! And then — he cried ——

MARIE.

[*Triumphantly.*] He cried? George cried? Have
you ever seen him do that before?

GERTRUDE.

No, never!

MARIE.

[*To herself.*]   He cried ——

GERTRUDE.

And then he said: " What if we should be parted, after all?"

MARIE.

If who should be parted — you and he?

GERTRUDE.

Yes — if he should die ——

MARIE.

If he — oh, that is what he meant!   Oh, well, he just wanted to say something.   [*With forced lightness.*]

GERTRUDE.

Of course he did.   But what about the other woman? Oh, I didn't let him see that I cared — and for the time I didn't care, really; but now, when I think of it!   My God! — if it were really so!   If I only knew!!!!!!!!

MARIE.

Of course, he would not tell you!

GERTRUDE.

Do you think he would tell any one else?

MARIE.

Yes, sooner than tell you.

GERTRUDE.

Yes! I suppose so!

MARIE.

Shall I ask him?

GERTRUDE.

Oh, if you would do that for me ——

MARIE.

There now, it is done.   Here is the comb and the rest of the hairpins.   Now go!

GERTRUDE.

And do you really think he would tell you?

MARIE.

I am sure he will.

GERTRUDE.

Oh, Marie, how grateful I shall be to you ——

MARIE.

[*Pushes her out of the door.*] Go now, go! [*Stretches herself.*] Ah — ah — ah —— [*Calls softly.*] George! [*There is a knock at the door.*] Come in!

PAUL.

[*Enters.*] Pardon me, Miss Marie; is Mr. Brauer in?

MARIE.

No, Mr. Paul!

PAUL.

The assistant pastor would like to speak to him — but here he is, himself.

PASTOR.

[*Enters.*] Good-morning, Miss Marie!

MARIE.

[*Offers her hand hesitatingly.*] Good-morning!

PASTOR.

I will wait here, Mr. Paul!

PAUL.

Then, Miss Marie, will you please give me the key to the cellar? I want to put the beer on the ice.

MARIE.

[*Gets key from keyboard.*] Here it is.

PAUL.

Thank you!

[*Exit.*]
[*Pause.*]

PASTOR.

And have you nothing to say to me?

MARIE.

What shall I say, Pastor?

PASTOR.

Are you not happy this day?

MARIE.

[*Hard.*] No!

PASTOR.

Not even on account of our betrothal?

MARIE.

We will have no betrothal, Pastor!

PASTOR.

What are you saying?

MARIE.

I shall leave this place ——

PASTOR.

You ——

MARIE.

To-day, I leave this house!

PASTOR.

Pardon me, if I have forced my attentions upon you ——

MARIE.

No! You have not!

PASTOR.

My attentions were honorable, I assure you ——

MARIE.

Thank you, Pastor, I know that; but ——

PASTOR.

Then it is not on my account you are leaving?

MARIE.

Certainly not!

PASTOR.

Does any one here know of your intention?

MARIE.

No one!

PASTOR.

Miss Marie, I am still a young man; if I should mention such a word as " life's happiness," it would, perhaps, sound absurd. . Therefore, I will not speak of myself. My fate is in my own hands. But if you realize this moment what you owe to this house — and I say this not for mine, nor for their sake, I say it for yours and yours alone; though I am but a poor mortal — it pains me — but be that as it may — Marie, if you cause a discord in this house, the blame will rest upon yourself.

MARIE.

Perhaps!

PASTOR.

Pardon me — I will not question you. I wish to know nothing; that, in the end, is always the best. Did I not love you as well as myself, I would not speak another word; but as matters stand now, I will say one —aye, one more word — I would not have dared to say otherwise. The greatest, the highest thing one possesses in this world, is his life's *melody* — a certain strain that ever vibrates, that his soul forever sings — waking or dreaming, loudly or softly, internally or externally. Others may say: " His temperament or his character is so, or so." He only smiles, for he knows his melody and he knows it alone. You see, Miss Marie, my life's happiness you have destroyed, but my life's melody you can not take from me.   That is pure and will always remain so.   And now I say to you, Miss Marie, if you fill this house, where you have obtained everything you possess— honor, bread, and love — if you fill this house with sorrow — if you dare to sin against your father and your mother ——

MARIE.

One moment, Pastor.   My father and my mother — what do you know about them? My father I don't know myself, but my mother? Ah yes, I know her well; and from her I have inherited my life's melody.   This melody has a beautiful text.   Do you want to know what it is, Pastor? It is, " *Thou shalt steal.*   Steal everything for thyself — thy life's happiness — thy love— all — all. Only others will enjoy it in the end."   Yes, Pastor, my mother is a thief.   On St. John's eve she came stealthily over yonder garden hedge; and as my mother, so am I!   And now, Pastor, ask me no more; I need all my senses, for to-day my entire happiness is at stake ! There — now you know all !

PASTOR.

Yes, now I know! Farewell, Miss Marie.   I will forget this day, perhaps ; *you* — never ——

[*Exit.*]

GERTRUDE.

[*Enters door L.*] Was that George, who just now left ?

MARIE.

Were you at that door, listening ?

GERTRUDE.

Marie! — For shame ! ! ! ! !

MARIE.

Now go and dress yourself; I will call George.   Go now, go !

[126]

GERTRUDE.

And will you come and tell me at once?

MARIE.

At once! Yes!! [GERTRUDE *exits*.] [MARIE *calling softly*.]   George! George!

GEORGE.

[*Enters from veranda*.]   Are you alone?

MARIE.

[*Nods*.]

GEORGE.

Have you arranged it so?

MARIE.

You wished to speak to me, so I have arranged it!

GEORGE.

Marie, I wished to tell you.   One hour more I am a free man — and my mind is made up.   It is yet time to change our fates.   What will you answer me?

MARIE.

Answer you?   Why, I don't know what you want.

GEORGE.

You know it well enough.   I want *you!*   Do you hear me?   *You*, who belong to me for life — I want you!

MARIE.

[*Softly — happily*.]   I thought the fires were out — and you had forgotten me — and now you want me?

GEORGE.

[*Softly*.]   Are you not mine?   Are you not my wife in the eyes of heaven?

MARIE.

Yes, but in the eyes of the world it is *Gertrude!*

GEORGE.

Must it, then, be so?

[127]

THE FIRES OF ST. JOHN

MARIE.

[*Doubtingly.*]   Go — go — you love her ——

GEORGE.

Yes, I do love her.   How could I help that?   Do you not also love her?

MARIE.

[*Bitterly.*]   Ah, I don't know.   A few moments ago, when I saw her in your arms — and you wept, too — only, because you love her!!   Oh, but I can bear it!!   I will bear it like — like — ah! ——   But there — that is no one's affair but mine ——

GEORGE.

So, so, that is no one's affair but yours, eh?   You might have invented a sweeter torture.   I meant to remain an honorable man all my life; if unable — well, there are plenty of bullets left.

MARIE.

And do you wish to die?

GEORGE.

I do not want to, I must!

MARIE.

George, then take me with you? [*He shakes his head.*] For years I have carried the wish in my heart — to kill you!   Then I would kiss and love you like mad — and then follow you into eternity ——

GEORGE.

Nonsense, girl, nonsense!   Can't you see, how one turns round and round and round in a circle, till at last to find no other escape than death?

MARIE.

I am not afraid to die; though with you, I'd rather live ——

THE FIRES OF ST. JOHN

GEORGE.

To live, dear, will require more courage for both of us.

MARIE.

How so?

GEORGE.

Can you ask? Here in this house, to which we owe everything — both you and I? Where they gave us food, shelter and love? After all that, would you have the courage to destroy their happiness?

MARIE.

The good old pastor used to say: "You must have the courage to do everything, except to do wrong." I would even have the courage to do wrong.

GEORGE.

Shall I put you to the test?

MARIE.

If you will give me your hand now and say to me: "Come, we will run away, through yonder garden gate — just as we are — now, this very moment" — you shall see how I will run!

GEORGE.

What? — Secretly — without telling any one? Is that what you mean?

MARIE.

Don't you?

GEORGE.

[*Laughs bitterly.*] No, no!

MARIE.

Well, what then?

GEORGE.

Face to face, like a man. There he stands — I here. If he will give me back my word, 'tis well. If he refuses [*determined*], 'tis also well.

THE FIRES OF ST. JOHN

MARIE.

My God! You know his temper! He will kill us —
he will kill us both!

GEORGE.

'Tis death either way ——

MARIE.

George — think ——

GEORGE.

Oh, I have thought of it for two days and two nights.
One is madness and the other insanity. There is no
other way. [*Pained.*] Only the thought of the child
gives me pain ——

MARIE.

Of course, if your feelings for Gertrude ——

GEORGE.

Then it is your desire? [*She nods assent.*] Very
well! So be it! But remember, it is a question of life
and death! — And, therefore, you yourself must be
present.

MARIE.

[*In terror.*] I? — I be present when you ask him?

GEORGE.

What? — You, who wish to become my helpmate and
partner in life, and share all my life's troubles —
you would desert me now — desert me in this hour? —
and I very much fear, not the worst in store for us?

MARIE.

No, no, George; it's not that — not that! But you
know how we have feared him and have trembled for
years — and now I should ——

GEORGE.

If you can't even do that ——

MARIE.

If necessary — yes! — I will do it.

GEORGE.

Then — as soon as he returns. [BRAUER *is heard breathing heavily*.] Ah, here he is!

BRAUER.

[*Enters*.] Why, that is almost an old-time Biblical miracle. Just think, children, think of it —— But where is Gertrude? Well? Can't you speak?

MARIE.

[*Trembling*.] I think she is dressing!

BRAUER.

Well, it will interest you also, so listen: I met the assistant pastor as he came from the house here, and he told me, rather piqued, that our good old pastor had suddenly risen from his bed and limpingly insisted upon delivering the wedding discourse himself. Well — what's the matter? Aren't you glad?

GEORGE.

H'm ——

BRAUER.

Of course, you are a perfect heathen! But I say, our assistant pastor must have been terribly put out. He had been preparing for that same address for days. He looked rather crestfallen; but then, there is no help for it.

GEORGE.

Pardon me, uncle; in order to save time, I must ask you for an interview.

BRAUER.

What, again? Can't you wait till afternoon?

GEORGE.

No! Before the ceremony, if you please.

BRAUER.

[*Startled.*] Wha — oh, I see. I suppose now you will demand more than I am willing to give? Marie, leave us —— [PAUL *enters.*] Well, what now?

PAUL.

[*Gives him a sign.*]

BRAUER.

There, look at him! Well, have you lost your tongue, man? Why don't you speak?

PAUL.

No, no, Mr. Brauer, I have something to say to you — alone.

BRAUER.

Then why don't you come nearer?

PAUL.

[*Whispering.*] We have just now caught the old woman.

BRAUER.

[*With a glance at* MARIE.] What? Marie, you may remain and chat with George for awhile; he is a very interesting young man. [*Softly, to* PAUL.] Where?

PAUL.

Down in the cellar; just as I wanted to put the beer on the ice, I found her there in a dark corner, loaded down with plunder!

BRAUER.

Is she there now?

PAUL.

Yes, struggling like a demon.

BRAUER.

Undoubtedly this offense will earn her a good long term in prison and we will be rid of her for a long time! But how to get her out of the house?

PAUL.

Leave that to me Mr. Brauer; I know a way to keep her quiet.

BRAUER.

Yes, yes, and in the meantime I will make out the papers and we will hand her over to the Gendarme; that will be the best. Children, I will be busy for a moment! Wait here until I return.

GEORGE.

Don't forget, uncle!

BRAUER.

No, no. I'll be back in a moment. Come, Mr. Paul!

[*Both exit.*]

GEORGE.

You are trembling ——

MARIE.

Am I?

GEORGE.

Marie dear, I am with you. No one shall harm you!

MARIE.

Oh, it is not that.

GEORGE.

What, then?

MARIE.

Oh, I don't know. It has suddenly come over me so —— [*Starts.*] Sh! He's coming!

[*Noise. Scuffling of feet and smothered cries are heard.*]

[133]

GEORGE.

What is it?

MARIE.

In God's name, be still!

GYPSY.

[*Calling for help.*] Mine daughter! Mine Mamie!
My Mamie!!

MARIE.

Hear? Hear? *My mother!* They are taking her
away — to prison! Sh! Be still! No, no; don't open
the door! Be quiet! Be quiet!

GYPSY.

[*Not as loud as before.*] Oh, mine daughter! My
Mamie — my Mamie ——!   [*Dying out.*]

GEORGE.

Will you not go out to her, no matter what she has
done?

MARIE.

How can I? How can I? I am afraid — afraid ——

GEORGE.

Then shall I go?

MARIE.

[*Frightened.*] No, no; don't leave me!! Sh! Be
quiet! So, quiet! Now they have gone! Thank
heaven! [*Again wailing, but very distant.*] Hear?
Hear? Let her shriek! Let her call! I cannot help
her! I am a thief, the same as she. I, too, have
come to this house, and I have stolen. But oh, my
God, what have I stolen? What have I stolen?

GEORGE.

Come, Marie, control yourself! Think of what we
have before us!

MARIE.

Yes, yes — I'll be quiet! What have we before us?
No, no; I will not — I cannot — I ——

GEORGE.

Do you mean to ——

BRAUER.

[*In door.*] Did you hear anything, children? Any
noise?

GEORGE.

We heard screams and a scuffle. What was the
matter?

BRAUER.

Oh, nothing of any consequence. Don't mind it.
An old vagabond of a woman, that's all. I have only
to sign the papers now, then I'll be back.   [*Exit.*]

GEORGE.

Marie!

MARIE.

Hush, not a word, not a word! She out there must
go her way, and I must go mine!

GEORGE.

What do you mean?

MARIE.

You said it yourself. 'Tis madness! Yes, yes; 'tis
madness! *All — all!* What we do — what we desire —
all — all!

GEORGE.

Marie!

MARIE.

Or do you imagine for one moment we could be
happy together? No, I know you too well. I know
the certain result. You would never forgive yourself

[135]

nor me, and in the end life would become a burden to me, if only because I was in your way. Yes, yes, that would be the end of it all ——

GEORGE.

Marie, I will be faithful to you forever, let come what may, be it good or bad; you know that!

MARIE.

Yes, thank God! — yes!

GEORGE.

If there was only the slightest possibility of a chance to escape from all this whirl — then we might be free, we might —— But no matter what we begin, we cannot shake off nor disregard our obligations to this house; never, as long as we live!

MARIE.

Therefore, what more can you desire? Everything . on earth we possess, all that was beautiful, all the love, all — all, we gave to each other. There is nothing more to give, for either one of us. St. John's night is past, the fires are out, are dead ——

GEORGE.

And what shall become of us?

MARIE.

Of you? That I can't tell. Perhaps you will be happy, perhaps not; that must all rest with yourself. And I? Oh, be content. I will take care of myself. As soon as possible I shall leave this house. Not to-day, as I would like — it might create suspicion ——

GEORGE.

And where will you go?

THE FIRES OF ST. JOHN

MARIE.

Ah, the world is large. I shall go far, far away, where no one will ever find me. No, no, not even you, George.

GEORGE.

And if you should go to ruin out there?

MARIE.

Do not fear. I am the calamity child, the foundling. My hands are hard and callous — see, see! Just like my heart is, now. I will work and work, and toil, until I fall exhausted — then I will sleep and rest, until it is time for work again; and thus I will perhaps maintain a miserable existence.

GEORGE.

You say you are a calamity child! Well, so am I. But our accounts do not harmonize. You are going out into the world and misery, and it was I who drove you to it. Even did I not love you as I do, that thought would follow me forever and embitter my entire life. But, be it so. We are both children of misery! Therefore let us grit our teeth, shake each other by the hand — and say farewell!

MARIE.

[*Softly.*] Good-bye, Georgie dear — and — don't be afraid — he is not yet coming — and forgive me — do you hear? From to-day — you understand? Did I not love you as much as I do, this would not have been quite so hard; but there — there — 'tis all right now — I know; I can never be entirely poor now; for once, at least, the fires of St. John have burned for me — once — just once ——

[137]

GEORGE.

Marie ——

MARIE.

[*Glancing around.*] Don't — don't ——

MRS. BRAUER.

[*Enters, followed by* GERTRUDE.] Hasn't the carriage arrived yet, children? And where is papa? It is time to go.

MARIE.

He is coming now, I believe.

BRAUER.

[*Enters.*] So there, I am ready to go! But, that is, you wanted to speak to me first?

GEORGE.

[*With a glance at* MARIE.] It is all settled now, thank you.

BRAUER.

Then come, wife, my coat, quick!
    [*She helps him with frock, after he has divested
      himself of jacket.*]

GERTRUDE.

[*Aside to* MARIE.] Did you ask him?

MARIE.

[*Nods.*]

GERTRUDE.

And what did he say?

MARIE.

It was all nonsense, my pet. He loves you and only you. He never has loved any one else — he says — and he will be very happy — so he says ——

GERTRUDE.

[*Embraces him joyfully.*] My darling George ——

[138]

THE FIRES OF ST. JOHN

BRAUER.

Come, come, my child — time enough for that after the ceremony.   Come!

> [*All follow him to the door. When* GEORGE *reaches door he turns, and as he takes one parting glance at* MARIE, BRAUER *pushes him off.* MARIE *stands motionless, looking after them, handkerchief in mouth, nervously forcing it between her teeth.*]

> [*Curtain.*]

END OF PLAY.